CW00956688

MC
DiVINE

St. Paschal Baylon
1540–1592
Patron of the Confraternity of the Blessed Sacrament

MOMENTS DIVINE

BEFORE THE BLESSED SACRAMENT

*Historic And Legendary Readings
And Prayers*

By

FR. FREDERICK A. REUTER, K.C.B.S.

TAN BOOKS AND PUBLISHERS, INC.
Rockford, Illinois 61105

Nihil Obstat: J. M. Corrigan, D.D.
                      Censor Librorum

Imprimatur: ✠ D. Cardinal Dougherty
                      Archbishop of Philadelphia
                      Philadelphia
                      July 1, 1922

Library of Congress Catalog Card No.: 95-61019

ISBN: 0-89555-533-6

Printed and bound in the United States of America.

TAN BOOKS AND PUBLISHERS, INC.
P.O. Box 424
Rockford, Illinois 61105
1995

ACKNOWLEDGMENTS

———

The author wishes to express his gratitude to Rev. Martin J. Scott, S.J., for useful matter and to Mr. J. P. Egan, LL.D., for valuable suggestions.

FREDERICK A. REUTER, K.C.B.S.

IMPORTANT NOTE

Receiving Holy Communion Worthily*

What is necessary to receive Holy Communion worthily?

1) You have to be a baptized Catholic;
2) have no mortal sin on your soul;
3) be fasting.

Do you have to go to Confession first every time you receive Communion?

No, unless you have mortal sin on your soul.

What kind of sin is it to receive Communion unworthily?

To do so knowingly and willingly is a mortal sin called a sacrilege.

> "Therefore whosoever shall eat this bread, or drink the chalice of the Lord unworthily, shall be guilty of the body and of the blood of the

Lord. But let a man prove himself: and so let him
eat of that bread, and drink of the chalice. For
he that eateth and drinketh unworthily, eateth
and drinketh judgment to himself, not discern-
ing the body of the Lord." (*1 Corinthians*
11:27-29).

What does "fasting" mean?

"Fasting" means that, for one hour before
receiving Communion, you have to stop
eating solid food and drinking all liquids
except water.

> You may take water, and if sick, medicine any
> time before receiving. You must stop chewing
> gum at least one hour before. Until the 1950's,
> the Church required fasting from midnight
> before Communion; this rule was later short-
> ened to three hours for food and one hour for
> liquids (with water being allowed at any time);
> then it was changed to one hour for food and
> drink, except water. It is very praiseworthy to
> continue observing the traditional fast either
> from midnight or for three hours.

---

*From *A Brief Catechism for Adults,* by Fr. William J. Cogan,
TAN, 1958/1993, pp. 79-80.

CONTENTS

INTRODUCTION

"If Jesus were better known in the Blessed Sacrament, earth would be brighter and Heaven nearer." This quotation sets forth the object of this book. Our Divine Master is ready to bestow innumerable graces through this Sacrament, which is also the outpouring of His Sacred Heart, and which are lost in consequence of the ignorance and indifference of men. When the Most Holy Sacrament is not revered and loved, scandals will abound, faith will languish, and the Church will mourn. On the other hand, if this Sacrament is worthily and frequently received, peace will reign in Christian hearts, the devil will lose power, and souls will be sanctified—"as many as received Him, to them He gave power to be made the sons of God."

I address myself not only to the faithful, who find all delight, comfort and help in their belief, but also to the indifferent ones of the world who must learn what precious joys are tasted and shared at the table of the God of peace, the God of love, of Him who cries out to us from His earthly tabernacles, "Come to Me. I am in the midst of you, and you know Me not...Come! I am the way, the truth and the life...Oh, if you only knew the gift of God...!"

Should this little work, a labor of love, with joy in the making, dispel the indifference and ignorance, and help sanctify the soul of even one of God's sons or daughters, it should, it would seem, make it dear to all lovers of the Eucharistic God, and fulfill the aim of the author.

The Sacred Heart Readings are taken from Abbe Berlioux, *Month of the Sacred Heart,* published in Paris, 1885. All indulgenced prayers are taken from the new *Raccolta.*

Declaration. In obedience to the decree of Urban VIII of holy memory, I declare that I do not attribute any but purely human authority to the miracles, revelations, graces and incidents contained in this work.

FREDERICK A. REUTER, K.C.B.S.
Mt. St. Dominic Academy
Caldwell, New Jersey
Feast of the Assumption, 1922

MOMENTS
DIVINE

READING 1

Story of the Blessed Sacrament
(Montreal, Canada—1807)

LONG YEARS ago, a young American girl journeyed from her home in Vermont to a convent in Montreal. She had read about nuns and had a great desire to see for herself what a convent was like. She was a Protestant and her people were not too well pleased at her request, but they granted it. She would learn much in the convent, they said. Other Protestant girls had finished their education in convents; why not Fanny?

So one day Fanny went to the door of the old Congregation Convent in the heart of Montreal. The portress admitted her and the good religious welcomed her most tenderly.

Weeks passed; Fanny was not happy. She

mocked openly at the rites she could not understand. The children wondered much, and fearing that they would be scandalized, the Reverend Mother decided to send the young girl back to her people in Vermont.

Among the Sisters was one who had a deep attachment for the Protestant pupil. She longed to bring her into the fold, and make her life satisfied and happy.

"I grieve to send the child home," said Mother, "but she does not improve and there is nothing else to be done."

"Give her another trial, dear Mother," pleaded the Sister. "Let her stay with us a few more weeks. God and His Blessed Mother may change her heart."

The Superior granted the petition and again was disappointed in the result. The last day of Fanny's probation was drawing near. It was September 8, the feast of the Nativity of the Blessed Virgin Mary.

Fanny spent the afternoon with the teacher she loved, but there was nothing in her conduct to show a change of spirit. She was still a doubter and spoke her thoughts in words that deeply grieved the religious. Yet Fanny helped to prepare the flowers for the altar, for Benediction of the Blessed Sacrament.

The Sister lifted the vase and was about to take it to the chapel, when something made her pause.

"Why not send Fanny? Fanny, the unbeliever!" Turning to the young girl she bade her take the vase and place it on the altar. "Be sure," added the Sister, "to adore Our Lord when you are there."

Fanny laughed and went away with the flowers. She did not believe. Why should she bow before the altar? In her home town Catholics were called idolaters. She would not become one. Thinking thus she reached the gate of the sanctuary, opened it, but could go no farther. She made another effort and yet her feet seemed powerless to move. For the third time she tried, only to fail; and then, overcome by awe and a strange compelling influence, she fell upon her knees and said her act of faith, the first she had ever made. Her God was present in the tabernacle, and there, humbled and ashamed, she knelt for some time. Then rising, she approached the altar and placed her fragrant flowers before the Blessed Sacrament.

Fanny's conversion was complete. "After such a miracle," she said, "I must give myself to my Saviour."

There was bitter opposition to overcome, but at last her mother yielded, and accompanied her daughter to Montreal, where, in the chapel of the Hotel-Dieu, Fanny realized that her lifework was to be among those holy women.

High above the altar a picture of the Holy Family looked down upon the Americans. "See, dear mother, Saint Joseph wants me here," said Fanny, and there she found absolute content.

Wonderful are the ways that our dear Lord opens to His children to find their true home. As we read the story of the "First American Nun," our hearts are stirred by the divine mercy that gave to Fanny Allen the grace to become a Catholic and a devoted religious.

Fanny Allen was born November 13, 1784, at Westminster, Vermont, and she died of lung trouble, at Hotel-Dieu, Montreal, December 10, 1819. Her father was General Ethen Allen, the patriot; he professed no religious belief.[1,2]

---

1. *Sacred Heart Review,* vol. 59, No. 9, 1918. *Cath. Encyc.,* vol. 1, p. 320.
2. A letter: Hotel-Dieu of St. Joseph, Montreal, Canada, July 16, 1919. *(See next page.)*

Glory be to God on high; and to Thee, O Jesus, on earth be all honor and adoration in the Blessed Sacrament forevermore! Amen.

Prayer

Dearest lord! Make us remember, when the world is cold and dreary and we know not where to turn for comfort, that

---

Reverend Father: Your kind favor of the 9th instant affords me the greatest pleasure in being able to forward to you the desired information concerning the marvelous story of Fanny Allen.

From our Annals we find that the youthful convert was born in Westminster, Vt., on Nov. 13th, 1784; entered the boarding school of the Sisters of the Congregation of Notre Dame in 1807; being 23 years of age.

Miss Allen was admitted in our cloister Sept. 29th, 1808 and ended her life by a most holy death, Dec. 10th, 1819.

The facts related in the "Sacred Heart Review" are found in accordance with what is recorded of our saintly Sister in the Annals of the Community, and also with the short sketch of her life written by the late Rt. Rev. L. de Goesbriand, first Bishop of Burlington, Vt., in the Catholic Memoirs of Vermont and New Hampshire.

Your humble servant,
Sister M. Theresa.

there is always *one spot* bright and cheerful
—the Sanctuary. When we are in *desolation
of spirit;* when all who are dear to us have
passed away, like summer flowers, and none
are left to love us and care for us, whisper
to our troubled souls that there is *one friend*
who dies not—one whose love never
changes—Jesus on the altar.

When *sorrows thicken* and crush us with
their burden, when we look in vain for
comfort, let Thy dear words come forth
with full force from the tabernacle: "Come
to Me all ye who labor and are heavily burdened, and I will refresh ye." Thy friendship,
dearest Lord, henceforth shall be the dearest
treasure we possess. It shall compensate for
the treachery and ingratitude of creatures.

It shall be our consolation when the wild
flowers are growing over the best-loved
ones, and when all who hold a dear place
in our hearts are withered and gone. With
Thy friendship the world shall never be
dreary, and life never without a charm.
Would that we could realize the pure happiness of possessing Thy sympathy. Would
that we could feel—when we are *crushed and
humbled*—when the hope we have lived for
has withered—when sorrows and trials that

we dare not reveal to any, make our souls sick well nigh unto death—when we look in vain for someone to understand us, one who will enter into our miseries, make us remember that there is One on the altar who knows *every fiber* of our hearts, *every sorrow,* every pain special to our peculiar natures, and who deeply sympathizes with us, and to suffer seems nothing to the bitterness of suffering alone.—*Fr. Augustine.*

Act of Contrition

O MY GOD I am heartily sorry for having offended Thee, because Thou art infinitely good and infinitely worthy of love, and because sin displeases Thee. I am firmly resolved, with the help of Thy grace, never to sin again.

Spiritual Communion

MY JESUS, I believe that Thou art present in the most Blessed Sacrament. I love Thee above all things, and I desire to receive Thee into my soul. Since I cannot now receive Thee sacramentally, come at least spiritually into my heart. I embrace Thee as if Thou

wert already come, and unite myself wholly to Thee. Never permit me to be separated from Thee. Amen.

Anima Christi

SOUL OF CHRIST, be my sanctification;
Body of Christ, be my salvation;
Blood of Christ, fill all my veins;
Water of Christ's side, wash out my stains;
Passion of Christ, my comfort be;
O good Jesus, listen to me;
In Thy wounds I fain would hide;
Ne'er to be parted from Thy side;
Guard me should the foe assail me;
Call me when my life shall fail me;
Bid me come to Thee above,
With Thy Saints to sing Thy love,
World without end. Amen.

Ejaculations

HAIL, O true Body, born of the Virgin Mary, and which for man was sacrificed upon the Cross.

Be thou blessed, O holy Virgin, through whom we received the heavenly Bread that preserves and increases true life within us.

A Sacred Heart Reading

A PIOUS lady who died in 1860, at the age of thirty-two years, had a great devotion to the most holy hearts of Jesus, Mary and Joseph. She took a particular pleasure in often invoking the names of the Holy Family, and in teaching them to her little child when seated on her knee. In her joys and sorrows, she never wearied repeating the holy aspirations: *Jesus, Mary, Joseph.* Many a time were tears of devotion seen to fill her eyes, whilst she pronounced those blessed names. She appeared then in a sort of ecstasy, and her heart was inflamed with devotion to the Holy Family, whom she wished, she used to say, to love in the name of all hearts. During a long and painful illness with which she was seized, she frequently cried out: "Jesus, Mary, Joseph, when I have suffered sufficiently, call me to you!" Towards the end, being scarcely able to speak, she breathed but one name: "Jesus, Jesus." That name was her great consolation, her last cry of hope and farewell. At length after a lingering martyrdom, she gently expired, her hand on the head of her child to bless it, her eyes raised to Heaven and the name of Jesus on her lips. Oh, beautiful and precious death. O ever blessed names, Jesus, Mary, Joseph! O hearts burning with love and tenderness.[3]

Mᴀʏ the Heart of Jesus in the Most Blessed Sacrament be praised, adored and loved with grateful affection, at every moment, in all the tabernacles of the world, even to the end of time! Amen.

---

3. Abbe Berlioux, *Month of the Sacred Heart,* 1885.

READING 2

Story of the Blessed Sacrament (Philadelphia, U.S.A.—1875)

THE Reverend Father John P. Dunn, who died years ago in Philadelphia, often related the following strange incident of his own experience:

It was in the early years of his priesthood that Father Dunn was granted the touching proof of the secret workings of the Blessed Sacrament. He was summoned one day to the house of an Episcopalian minister, who was distinguished for his bitter hostilities to everything pertaining to "Romanism." Wondering a little at the summons, the good priest instantly went thither, expecting to be taken to the bedside of some faithful servant whose importunity for the rites of the

Church had triumphed over the bigotry of her employers. To his amazement, he was shown at once into an elegant chamber, where the minister's only child lay on her death bed. She was a fair and winning child of nine summers, the idol of the household, intelligent beyond her years. Blessed with perfect health and watched over with tenderest solicitude, she had bid fair to blossom into womanhood unmarked by pain or sorrow. Yet the little child had for nearly four years borne a secret sorrow which at last had brought her, without disease or accident, to the brink of the grave. There was nothing to grapple with, the doctors said; she was fading away before their eyes with no symptom of illness, no token of decline—only dying. The medical men studied the strange case with interest, friends wondered and wept, the parents grew stern and hardened in their grief. Well they knew what brought this precious little one to this condition.

On this day the family physician had caught the first clue for his guidance. It was a bitter exclamation against "Popish servant girls" which broke from the lips of the mother, as with wild, tearless eyes she gazed upon her fading flower. The doctor demanded an explanation of her words, sternly reminding her that he had a right to know the cause of the child's strange illness. Her reluctance being finally overcome, the mother began by stating that they had once been unhappily persuaded to engage an Irish Catholic girl as the attendant of their little Lena. The girl was far superior to her station, and in fact they treated her almost as one of the family, little thinking they were cherishing a viper. They had strong hopes of her conversion, for she never went to church, had no popish book or emblem of any sort, and was really so indifferent about religion that they were convinced that she had not the slightest recollection of the "superstitions" of her native country. They had not striven to hasten her conversion, believing that the attention she gave to their instructions to the child, at which she was generally present, was sowing the seed.

One afternoon she took Lena out for her usual walk and, for the first time in years, according to her own statement afterwards, she felt an inclination to go to church. It was a day on which "Benediction" was given, and from that fatal day dated all their misery. The child was so impressed by the ceremonies that she longed to go again. From a most pious, docile disposition, she became disobedient and stubborn, no longer taking any interest in her prayers or her Bible lessons, and at divine service showing none of her former reverence and thoughtful attention. Of course the faithless servant was dismissed without delay and the little victim of her diabolical art surrounded with all good influences. But in vain, the child longed and pined after the popish ceremony, and the terrible infatuation or possession, whichever it might be, was destroying her life.

The physician's comment on the story was an instant command that a Catholic priest should be brought to his patient, and he suggested Father Dunn, whom he had often met. Despite the opposition of the mother, the young priest was called in. The child had heard nothing of this. The Protestant doctor imagined the priest would go through some ceremony that would rouse her to animation, and he watched anxiously from the door. To his amazement the child sprang up in bed at the instant the priest entered the room, and with clasped hands and eager gaze awaited his approach. "You have brought my Lord!" she cried in a voice at once pathetic and exulting. "I wouldn't go without Him."

Father Dunn's surprise was as great as the doctor's. He tried to soothe and divert her, but she put her little wasted hand on his breast, where the Blessed Sacrament rested, and by her answers to the questions showed that she was as thoroughly familiar as himself with the great Mystery. "Gratify her, my dear sir—her life is at stake!" urged the anxious doctor. The young priest knew better than the aged physician, but he hesitated no longer. The innocent child made her act of contrition and love as he prompted, received her Lord, and with a happy smile sank back into the pillow. As Father Dunn gave the blessing the seraphic soul fled to its Love.[1]

MY soul thirsteth after the living God. When may I come to this wonderful tabernacle, the house of my God!

---

1. *Glimpses of the Supernatural,* p. 95. *Sentinel of the Blessed Sacrament,* vol. XXII, p. 10.

Prayer

O JESUS, here present in the Holy Eucharist, Thy Heart is all aglow with love for me! Thou dost call me, Thou dost urge me to come to Thee, yea, more: Thou dost descend from Thy throne, Thou dost leave Thy tabernacle to enter my poor heart.

Thou dost crave to dwell in my heart. Ah, that I could prepare for Thee a fitting abode! Send forth the fire of Thy love and in Thy mercy make my cold, tepid heart burn for Thee. Amen.—*St. Ildephons.*

Act of Contrition

O MY GOD I am heartily sorry for having offended Thee, because Thou art infinitely good and infinitely worthy of love, and because sin displeases Thee. I am firmly resolved, with the help of Thy grace, never to sin again.

Spiritual Communion

MY JESUS, I believe that Thou art present in the most Blessed Sacrament. I love Thee

above all things, and I desire to receive Thee into my soul. Since I cannot now receive Thee sacramentally, come at least spiritually into my heart. I embrace Thee as if Thou wert already come, and unite myself wholly to Thee. Never permit me to be separated from Thee. Amen.

Anima Christi

SOUL OF CHRIST, be my sanctification;
Body of Christ, be my salvation;
Blood of Christ, fill all my veins;
Water of Christ's side, wash out my stains;
Passion of Christ, my comfort be;
O good Jesus, listen to me;
In Thy wounds I fain would hide;
Ne'er to be parted from Thy side;
Guard me should the foe assail me;
Call me when my life shall fail me;
Bid me come to Thee above,
With Thy Saints to sing Thy love,
World without end. Amen.

Ejaculation

O BELOVED SAVIOUR, my Jesus, I am Thine and will ever remain Thine. Come to me, O Jesus, Thou sweetest Manna, and satiate my inexpressibly great hunger.

A Sacred Heart Reading

NOT long ago, a zealous priest wrote as follows: Our work of the Communion of Reparation makes rapid progress and produces abundant fruit. The Communions of the associates are most efficacious in obtaining the conversion of sinners. An Englishman, a Protestant, who on account of ill health, had taken up his abode in my parish, was reduced to the last extremity. I visited him and endeavored to persuade him to embrace the Catholic Faith and thus secure his salvation. "I was born a Protestant," he replied, "and I shall die a Protestant." Despairing of converting him by arguments, I assembled the associates of the Communion of Reparation, and I implored them to ask most earnestly of the Sacred Heart of Jesus the conversion of this poor invalid, who was on the point of dying in heresy and impenitence. The associates offered their Communions and prayed much for him during that day, and when I went again to see him, he said, with a sweet smile:

"I am convinced of the truth, I will become a Catholic." He made his abjuration in the presence of several witnesses and received the Sacrament of Baptism with tears of joy. "Father," he said to me afterwards, "How happy and peaceful I feel; it seems as if I were returning to life." A few days after, he received the Holy Viaticum and Extreme Unction with sentiments of the tenderest piety, and the Archbishop administered to him the Sacrament of Confirmation. Is not this an example of the consoling fruits of the Communion of Reparation?

MAY the Heart of Jesus in the Most Blessed Sacrament be praised, adored and loved with grateful affection, at every moment, in all the tabernacles of the world, even to the end of time! Amen.

READING 3

Story of the Blessed Sacrament (Lourdes, France—1901)

THE Reverend Father Martin J. Scott, S.J., in his admirable book *The Hand of God*,[1] recounts the following miracle which happened at Lourdes, the famous shrine of the Blessed Mother of God:

"On the 17th of December, 1899, the fast mail on the way from Bordeaux to Paris met with a collision. In the mail car was a post office express clerk, Gabriel Gargan, thirty years old. At the time of the wreck the train was going at the speed of fifty miles an hour. By the crash Gargan was thrown fifty-two feet. He was terribly bruised and bro-

1. P. J. Kenedy & Sons, Publishers, New York.

20

ken and paralyzed from the waist down. He was barely alive when lifted onto a stretcher.

"Taken to a hospital, his existence for some time was a living death. After eight months he had wasted away to a mere skeleton, weighing but seventy-eight pounds, although normally a big man. His feet became gangrenous. He could take no solid food and was obliged to take nourishment by a tube. Only once in twenty-four hours could he be fed even that way.

"He brought suit for damages against the railroad. The Appellate Court confirmed the verdict of the former courts and granted him 6,000 francs annually, and besides, an indemnity of 60,000 francs.

"Gargan's condition was pitiable in the extreme. He could not help himself even in the most trifling needs. Two trained nurses were needed day and night to assist him. That was Gabriel Gargan as he was after the accident, and as he would continue to be until death relieved him. About his desperate condition there could be no doubt. The railroad fought the case on every point. There was no room for deception or hearsay. Two courts attested to his condition, and the final payment of the railroad left the case a matter of record. Doctors testified that the man was a hopeless cripple for life, and their testimony was not disputed.

"Previous to the accident Gargan had not been to church for fifteen years. His aunt, who was a nun of the Order of the Sacred Heart, begged him to go to Lourdes. He refused. She continued her appeals to him to place himself in the hands of Our Lady of Lourdes. He was deaf to all her prayers.

"After continuous pleading of his mother he consented to go to Lourdes. It was now two years since the accident, and not for a moment had he left his bed all that time. He was carried on a stretcher to the train. The exertion caused him to faint, and for a full hour he was unconscious. They were on the point of abandoning the pilgrimage, as it looked as if he would die on the way, but the mother insisted, and the journey was made.

"Arrived at Lourdes, he went to confession and received Holy Communion. There was no change in his condition. Later he was carried to the miraculous pool and tenderly placed in its waters—no effect. Rather a bad effect resulted, for the exertion threw him into a swoon and he lay apparently dead.

After a time, as he did not revive, they thought him dead. Sorrowfully they wheeled the carriage back to the hotel. On the way back they saw the procession of the Blessed Sacrament approaching. They stood aside to let it pass, having placed a cloth over the face of the man whom they supposed to be dead.

"As the priest passed carrying the Sacred Host, he pronounced Benediction over the sorrowful group around the covered body. Soon there was a movement from under the covering. To the amazement of the bystanders, the body raised itself to a sitting posture. While the family were looking on dumbfounded and the spectators gazed in amazement, Gargan said in a full, strong voice that he wanted to get up.

"They thought that it was a delirium before death, and tried to soothe him, but he was not to be restrained. He got up and stood erect, walked a few paces and said that he was cured. The multitude looked in wonder, and then fell on their knees and thanked God for this new sign of His power at the shrine of His Blessed Mother. As Gargan had on him only invalid's clothes, he returned to the carriage and was wheeled back to the hotel. There he was soon dressed, and proceeded to walk about as if nothing had ever ailed him. For two years hardly any food had passed his lips but now he sat down to the table and ate a hearty meal.

"On August 20th, 1901, sixty prominent doctors examined Gargan. Without stating the nature of the cure, they pronounced him entirely cured. Gargan, out of gratitude to God in the Holy Eucharist and His Blessed Mother, consecrated himself to the service of the invalids at Lourdes.

"Fifteen years after his miraculous cure he was still engaged in his strenuous and devoted work. He was for years a living, visible testimony of the supernatural. Lifting the helpless from their cots, aiding the cripples, ministering to the afflicted, he was to be seen day after day, a living miracle. He may be there yet, for I have not heard of his death, but millions have seen him and millions knew what he was before he came to Lourdes."

O JESUS, through a miracle of love, Thou givest me in the Holy Eucharist even Thy

Sacred Heart as a nourishment for my soul and as a pledge of Thy love.

Prayer

GREAT GOD, immortal God, King of all ages! Oh that all creatures in Heaven and on earth would make to Thee a solemn reparation of honor for all the sins committed in Thy presence against the Most Holy Sacrament of the altar, for the fury of so many heretics, the wickedness of so many freethinkers, the profanations and sacrileges of so many sinners.

With a lively faith and bitter grief, we humbly adore Thee in this Sacrament of Thy power and love. We will ever honor Thy adorable person by coming into Thy sacred presence with due reverence, and will strive to repair the outrages offered to Thee by loving and venerating Thee with all our hearts.—*St. Catherine of Siena.*

Act of Contrition

O MY GOD I am heartily sorry for having offended Thee, because Thou art infinitely good and infinitely worthy of love, and

because sin displeases Thee. I am firmly resolved, with the help of Thy grace, never to sin again.

Spiritual Communion

MY JESUS, I believe that Thou art present in the most Blessed Sacrament. I love Thee above all things, and I desire to receive Thee into my soul. Since I cannot now receive Thee sacramentally, come at least spiritually into my heart. I embrace Thee as if Thou wert already come, and unite myself wholly to Thee. Never permit me to be separated from Thee. Amen.

Anima Christi

SOUL OF CHRIST, be my sanctification;
Body of Christ, be my salvation;
Blood of Christ, fill all my veins;
Water of Christ's side, wash out my stains;
Passion of Christ, my comfort be;
O good Jesus, listen to me;
In Thy wounds I fain would hide;
Ne'er to be parted from Thy side;
Guard me should the foe assail me;
Call me when my life shall fail me;

Bid me come to Thee above,
With Thy Saints to sing Thy love,
World without end. Amen.

Ejaculations

O JESUS, in Thy presence I feel my unworthiness and sloth, and my many sins justly fill me with fear.

O Jesus, here Thou continuest to the end the life of divine Love; for this Thou willest to remain ever present in the Blessed Sacrament.

A Sacred Heart Reading

PARIS was besieged by the Prussian army; Rome had just fallen into the hands of the Piedmontese, and the Communists were plotting in secret their terrible plans. Who was there to come to the assistance of the Holy Father? Who was there to save France? Holy souls cried out: "It is the Sacred Heart of Jesus which will save us; let us make to It a national vow." And what was this national vow? It was a promise to offer in the name of the whole nation, the solemn expression of their repentance by raising a memorial church in Paris dedicated to the Sacred Heart. There is a spot in Paris which in former times was bedewed with the blood of St. Denis and his companions, called the Quarter of Montmartre, or the Hill of the Martyrs, and it is there that the memorial church was built. The national vow was addressed to the Sacred Heart, because this divine Heart is the highest expression of the love of God for men; and because France had in a particular manner wounded the Sacred Heart of Jesus, which has loved her so much. Alms were asked and the funds increased, and subscriptions flowed in from all sides, and the new Basilica was raised. On its principal front is engraved in letters of gold the following dedication: "Devoted and Repentant France, to Christ and His Sacred Heart."

MAY the Heart of Jesus in the Most Blessed Sacrament be praised, adored and loved with grateful affection, at every moment, in all the tabernacles of the world, even to the end of time! Amen.

READING 4

Story of the Blessed Sacrament (Slavings, Moravia—1220)

SOME hundred paces outside of the city of Slavings, in Moravia, the traveler may see an old church dedicated to the Holy Ghost. It is very near to a small monastery, which stands alone under the shelter of a wooded hill, removed from the noise and the bustle of the world.

In the annals of the Moravian church we find the story of the following remarkable event:

In the spring of the year 1220, it happened that on a certain stormy night the parish church of Slavings was broken into by robbers and the sacred vessels containing the Blessed Sacrament carried away. The

29

perpetrators of this sacrilege were not discovered, but great was the distress among the people on account of the dishonor to the Most Holy.

A few months after the robbery had been committed, it happened that a cowherd was pasturing his flock near the spot where the church now stands. Some farmers were laboring in the field nearby, when suddenly there appeared, out of the little heap of stones overgrown with bushes, a flame of fire. As the beasts that were grazing nearby saw this mysterious light they threw themselves on the ground, while the cowherd, full of astonishment, called to the nearest neighbor: "Fire, neighbors, fire!"

After a close examination of this singular occurrence, they found, to their joyful astonishment, the stolen Hosts lying among the stones, surrounded by a brilliant light. Then with all speed they sought the services of a priest who most carefully gathered up the Sacred Particles and reverently took them to the parish church. The townspeople formed a procession and amidst great rejoicings accompanied Our Lord to His tabernacle. But when the procession arrived at the city gate, tradition affirms that the

Most Holy Sacrament disappeared from the hands of the priest and returned to the spot where It had been found. Three times was this fact repeated, after which both priest and people, perceiving that Our Lord had chosen it for His dwelling place, unanimously resolved to build Him a church on the spot. After this solemn promise had been made the priest proceeded with the Sacred Particles to the parish church unmolested.

The news of the incident spread far and wide, drawing a great throng of the faithful to the locality. The shrine was richly indulgenced, first by Bishop Dietrich of Olmuetz, afterwards by Gregory, Bishop of Prague, and later by many other bishops.

Emperor Joseph, in the year 1783, had planned to pull the church down, but at the earnest petition of the people it was allowed to remain as an object of veneration, under the title of the Church of the Holy Ghost.

The little heap of stones may be seen to this day beneath the privileged altar which stands in the center of the church. The day on which the cowherd saw the miraculous fire is an anniversary by the name of the "Countryman's Firefeast."[1]

O MY JESUS, I adore Thee in this holy Sacrament as my Lord and my God, my Redeemer and Saviour.

Prayer

O DIVINE MASTER, meek and humble of heart! No, there is no hovel so wretched, no temple so poor, no sanctuary so unadorned wherein Thou dost refuse to dwell for us. There is no street so miserable through which Thou dost not pass, no hut so indigent to which Thou dost not repair, no invalid so repulsive that Thou dost not visit. Thou settest Thy tabernacle in the midst of us; Thou becomest one of us. Thou art not ashamed either of our poverty or our baseness, Thou dost not repulse any of our ministers, Thou comest to us wretched creatures as often as we please; Thou makest no exception of seasons, or months, or days, or moments of the day. To what an excess does Thy love incite Thee, to what a state of

---

1. Gaulbe, *Fastes et Legendes du S. Sacrament.* Ott, *Euch.,* p. 223. E. M. Shapcotte, *Eucharistic Hours.*

abjection does it reduce Thee, O King of Kings?

Astonishment and admiration deprive me of speech! O hidden God, were a cherub, clothed with our nature, to visit a poor cottage, were he to permit us to see and honor him, it would be a great favor! Were a seraph to make us the priceless present of the fringe of Thy robe it would be a magnificent gift; and yet not all that would satisfy the insatiable desires of our heart.

But that Thou, the Master of Heaven and earth, shouldst give Thyself entire, concealed under the weak species, on all altars, in all chalices, frequently laid on soiled and torn linen, not only to be adored but to be eaten by all men without distinction; not once, nor in one place only, but at all times in all places—this is a miracle so stupendous, so exalted, that it exhausts in some manner the efforts of Thine omnipotence, the inventions of Thy wisdom, and the tenderness of Thy love. At the sight of this adorable Mystery, in transports of gratitude we proclaim: "The Lamb is worthy to receive power, and divinity, and wisdom, and strength, and honor and glory and benediction." Amen.—*St. Thomas Aquinas.*

Act of Contrition

O MY GOD I am heartily sorry for having offended Thee, because Thou art infinitely good and infinitely worthy of love, and because sin displeases Thee. I am firmly resolved, with the help of Thy grace, never to sin again.

Spiritual Communion

MY JESUS, I believe that Thou art present in the most Blessed Sacrament. I love Thee above all things, and I desire to receive Thee into my soul. Since I cannot now receive Thee sacramentally, come at least spiritually into my heart. I embrace Thee as if Thou wert already come, and unite myself wholly to Thee. Never permit me to be separated from Thee. Amen.

Anima Christi

SOUL OF CHRIST, be my sanctification;
Body of Christ, be my salvation;
Blood of Christ, fill all my veins;
Water of Christ's side, wash out my stains;

Passion of Christ, my comfort be;
O good Jesus, listen to me;
In Thy wounds I fain would hide;
Ne'er to be parted from Thy side;
Guard me should the foe assail me;
Call me when my life shall fail me;
Bid me come to Thee above,
With Thy Saints to sing Thy love,
World without end. Amen.

Ejaculations

O JESUS, through a miracle of love, Thou givest me in the Holy Eucharist even Thy Sacred Heart as a nourishment for my soul and as a pledge of Thy love.

O King of angels, who can tell Thy worth? The angels around Thy tabernacle know how far too short eternity will prove to exhaust the wonders of Thy Sacrament of Love.

A Sacred Heart Reading

AT the recommendation of a Protestant family living in the town of Liege in Belgium, a young lady who had been long ill was received into the hospital. She was an excellent musician, had lived entirely amongst heretics, and although nominally a Catholic, had no idea of religion and scarcely believed in the existence of God, giving herself up to all the pleasures of the world. When anyone spoke to her of religion, she became irritable and declared that such conversations fatigued her. The nursing Sisters who were in charge of the hospital, despairing of her conversion, made a novena for her to the agonizing Heart of Jesus. On the last day of the novena, the poor sinner asked one of the Sisters for a prayer book and after reading a page exclaimed: "I will go to confession and Communion." She made her confession and Communion, and from that day she said to all who came to see her: "Oh! how truly happy I am." On the near approach of death she expressed a desire to communicate again, and during her agony she repeated with fervor the words: "My Saviour, my Saviour, forgive me all my sins," peacefully expiring with the Holy Name still on her lips. Thus was this poor soul saved by being recommended to the agonizing Heart of Jesus. Glory and love to this divine Heart.

MAY the Heart of Jesus in the Most Blessed Sacrament be praised, adored and loved with grateful affection, at every moment, in all the tabernacles of the world, even to the end of time! Amen.

READING 5

Story of the Blessed Sacrament (Amsterdam, Holland—1345)

IN the early days of the city of Amsterdam, one of the greatest attractions of the metropolis was the "Holy Room." The following recorded fact established the history of the building.

In the year 1345, a man who was a devout Catholic was taken seriously ill. He had expressed a desire to receive the last rites of the Church and, accordingly, his family notified the pastor of the church, known at the time as the "Old Church," but which at present is a Protestant house of worship.

The priest after giving Holy Viaticum to the sick man advised the family in case the patient should vomit immediately after receiving the Blessed Sacrament to throw the contents into the fire. This weakness of the sick man was known to the immediate members of the family, and so the attendants made ready a basin into which the patient later vomited. The contents of this dish were then thrown into the fire, which was burning in the grate located in the sick room. This happened on Tuesday, March the twelfth.

Early in the morning of the following day, while one of the women was raking the fire with the poker, she saw in the center of the grate the Blessed Sacrament in the form of bread, surrounded by a halo of light. The woman was very much disturbed, and putting her hand into the fire she actually rescued the Host without burning herself. To her surprise she found the Host cold. The woman at once called in one of her neighbors and showed her the Blessed Sacrament which she had taken out of the fire, requesting the latter to take It to her home. Thus requested, the woman placed the Host on a clean cloth and locked It in a box. Shortly after, the husband of the original finder heard about the event and was very desirous of seeing the Host. As he was about to take It into his hand, however, the Sacred Particle seemed to resist—as if It did not want to be touched by the hands of a man. The priest was summoned at once and placed the Host in a pyx, but, strange to relate, when he tried to wash the cloth upon which the Sacred Host had rested, and returned to the chest in which he had locked the treasure, he found the pyx upset and the Host had disappeared.

The next morning the woman on opening the chest found the Blessed Sacrament on a clean cloth resting on a cushion. Without delay she called the pastor of the church, who placed the Sacred Host in the tabernacle. A few days later, indeed, the woman again found the Host in the chest. There was then no doubt this time that it was God's holy will that the miracle should be made known.

The priest informed the clergy of Amsterdam, who assembled and in a solemn procession carried the Sacred Host to the church. The home of the sick man was soon converted into a chapel, from which, as early as 1360, public processions were organized and pilgrimages were instituted.

On May 25, 1452, a large conflagration broke out, which reduced three-quarters of the city to ruins. It was during this time that the chapel, which was called the "Holy

Room," became a prey to the flames. Strange
to say, the monstrance containing the miraculous Host, which had been brought from
the "Old Church," was spared.

In the year of 1456, a new "Holy Room"
was built, and surrounding it a beautiful
church, 185 feet long and 130 feet wide, had
been erected. Many pilgrimages came to
Amsterdam to visit the shrine. Archduke
Maximilian, later on Roman Emperor, came
in the year 1480 to ask God for a cure, and
in commemoration of his recovery through
prayer, he caused a beautiful window to be
placed in the "Holy Room." He also gave
the city of Amsterdam the right of crowning
the emperors over the escutcheon of the city,
a privilege which the city of Amsterdam
enjoys to the present day.

The second half of the sixteenth century
was the beginning of most sorrowful days
for the Catholics of Amsterdam. Protestant-
ism made great inroads, churches and statues
were destroyed, and even the "Holy Room"
fell into the hands of the vandals. The persecution went so far as to prohibit public
processions. Nevertheless, the faithful continued to go quietly to the nearby church,
which had been spared by the Protestants.

In this church on March 12, the feast of the miraculous Host is celebrated. To this very day, the Catholics of Amsterdam go quietly in procession on the Sunday following March 12. Not only the people of the city, but also the devout fishermen of Volkendam, go in large numbers.

The "Holy Room" has not been used as a chapel since 1910, for in spite of the offer of the Catholics to buy it, the Protestant council permitted the "Holy Room" to be torn down, thus depriving Amsterdam of one of its most historic buildings. But the devotion of the Catholics has rather increased, for every year a larger number go there in procession, walking in groups of forty or fifty through the streets in the neighborhood of the former "Holy Room" as early as four o'clock in the morning. At the end of their walk they go into the adjacent church and receive Holy Communion.[1]

JESUS, Thou dwellest in the Sacred Mystery of Thy love for the love of me and to comfort me and sanctify me by Thy love.

---

1. *Cath. Encyc.,* vol. I, p. 441d. Milkamp, *Holy Room* (1860). *Emmanuel,* 1917.

Prayer

O MYSTERY worthy of the admiration of angels! Mystery, Whose excellence is infinitely enhanced by the end which the King of glory proposes to Himself in reducing Himself to so abject a condition! This truly hidden God has withdrawn into the obscurity of His Tabernacle to console the afflicted, sustain the tempted, enrich the indigent, protect the unfortunate, heal the sick and load with benefits all those who visit Him.

My God, we believe in this excess of love, and yet we languish in a degrading tepidity. We requite such matchless tenderness with the darkest ingratitude. Culpable that we are, we know, O great God, that Thou art present on the altar, and yet we sin in every possible way against the respect which is due Thee. The angels tremble in Thy presence, the princes of the heavenly court humble themselves into the abyss of their nothingness. It is we alone, vile insects that we are, who dare to appear before Thy tremendous Majesty in an irreverent posture. Thou invitest us to Thy adorable Banquet, but we are desirous only of perishable food, and receive without desire the Bread of Angels.

O Divine Son, veiled under the sacramental species! Melt, I implore Thee, this icy heart of mine, and inflame it with the sacred fire of Thy Love, that it may be a fiery furnace before Thy tabernacle whence the incense of fervor may perpetually ascend to Thee. Amen.—*Fenelon.*

Act of Contrition

O MY GOD I am heartily sorry for having offended Thee, because Thou art infinitely good and infinitely worthy of love, and because sin displeases Thee. I am firmly resolved, with the help of Thy grace, never to sin again.

Spiritual Communion

MY JESUS, I believe that Thou art present in the most Blessed Sacrament. I love Thee above all things, and I desire to receive Thee into my soul. Since I cannot now receive Thee sacramentally, come at least spiritually into my heart. I embrace Thee as if Thou

wert already come, and unite myself wholly to Thee. Never permit me to be separated from Thee. Amen.

Anima Christi

Soul of Christ, be my sanctification;
Body of Christ, be my salvation;
Blood of Christ, fill all my veins;
Water of Christ's side, wash out my stains;
Passion of Christ, my comfort be;
O good Jesus, listen to me;
In Thy wounds I fain would hide;
Ne'er to be parted from Thy side;
Guard me should the foe assail me;
Call me when my life shall fail me;
Bid me come to Thee above,
With Thy Saints to sing Thy love,
World without end. Amen.

Ejaculations

My saviour, sprinkle me with Thy Precious Blood, and lead me in the way of Thy Passion, and keep me beneath the shadow of the Cross, that I may come near Thine altar seeking Thee.

O most holy Jesus, give me an upright

and a just heart, that I may love "Thee, the King of Jerusalem, and wait for Thy coming, and feed upon the Bread of Life."

A Sacred Heart Reading

HISTORY relates that the Tartars, having spread terror throughout Europe, besieged with a large army Kinwalous, the capital of European and Asiatic Russia. After a vigorous resistance, the city was taken by assault and sacked by the enemy who, having massacred great numbers of the inhabitants, finally set fire to it. When the victorious army entered the town, St. Hyacinth, a Dominican monk, was at the altar saying Mass: his religious brethren came and warned him that there was not a moment to lose, and that if he wished to save himself and his community it was necessary to fly at once, otherwise he would fall into the hands of the barbarians. He followed their advice, but unwilling to leave the Holy Eucharist exposed to the profanations of the enemy, he took in one hand the ciborium and in the other the image of the Blessed Virgin, saying to his religious: "Follow me, my brethren, and be full of confidence; the

Sacred Heart of Jesus in the Blessed Sacrament and the Immaculate Heart of Mary will save us." He left the church followed by the community, went through the burning streets and passed by the hordes of barbarians, who gazed on him with respect and admiration. Reaching the banks of the river Borysthenus and not finding any boat there, he recommended himself to Jesus and Mary, and stepping on the water which remained firm beneath him, he crossed the river with dry feet, accompanied by all his brethren, and thus they were saved! O Christian! Receive the divine Host into your heart, place upon your breast the image of Mary and you will triumph over all the enemies of your salvation. Heart of Jesus, Heart of Mary, be always our hope, our love, our refuge and our salvation.

MAY the Heart of Jesus in the Most Blessed Sacrament be praised, adored and loved with grateful affection, at every moment, in all the tabernacles of the world, even to the end of time! Amen.

READING 6

Story of the Blessed Sacrament
(Erding, Bavaria—1497)

THE PELICAN, a Bavarian publication of recent years, brought to the notice of the public in the year 1886 the following marvelous occurrence which happened at Erding, a small town in Bavaria:

In the year 1497, two residents of the town of Erding, the one a wealthy citizen, the other a poor peasant, began conversing about their different conditions in life. The former, a God-fearing man, was asked by the latter to explain how it happened that he was always so lucky in his undertakings, whilst he himself was so unfortunate in everything he attempted. "Know this," replied the rich man, "that I possess a great secret treasure which I keep most carefully; as long as I retain this no evil can befall me." "And what is this treasure?" the poor man eagerly inquired. "The Blessed Sacrament," was the reverent reply. By this the latter meant that the frequent reception of Jesus in the Holy Eucharist was the source of all his good fortune. But the other, ignorant of this meaning, straightway formed a plan by which he might secure the Blessed Sacrament, that it might be his talisman also.

It happened to be Holy Thursday, and the peasant with the rest of the faithful approached the altar railing to receive Holy Communion. No sooner had the Sacred Host been given him than he removed It from his mouth and placed It in a clean napkin he had in his pocket. He meant no harm and acted from ignorance rather than from malice, yet he was fretful, nevertheless, fearing that God would punish him for the deed. On his way home he was frustrated in his plan, for he had already passed without the city when the Sacred Host freed Itself from the covering, and rising in the air, remained suspended there for a little while and then gradually lowered Itself to the ground and disappeared. With tears in his eyes, the poor man returned to the church and told his pastor and the entire congregation of his sacrilegious act. All immediately hurried to the spot, and behold, the Host lifted Itself from the ground, hovered in the air for a time and then descended and was lost to view!

The incident having been reported to the Bishop of Freesing, he and his cathedral chapter visited the place in order to make a thorough investigation. An immense concourse of people followed him to the spot. Again did the consecrated Particle raise Itself from the ground, and evading the outstretched hands that tried to secure It, moved to and fro, till It descended into the earth and vanished. Falling on their knees, the faithful remained prostrate in wonderment and fear, but soon the full signification of the miracle dawned upon them. "The Lord has sanctified this spot," they said; "here He wishes to dwell, and here we shall erect a sanctuary to atone for the sacrilege."

It was not long ere plans were drawn up for the construction of a church dedicated to the Precious Blood. Pilgrims came from all parts of the world and deemed themselves happy if they were only permitted to take a little of the soil as a relic, or drink of a nearby spring which seemed to have been endowed with healing powers. Pope Sixtus IV, having received an authentic account of the miracle, granted indulgences to the pilgrims visiting the place, both the diocesan bishop and a large number of people having testified to the truth of the miraculous occurrence.

It has been said before that this poor man, the perpetrator of the sacrilege, acted out of ignorance rather than malicious intent, yet we see that God, nevertheless, demanded satisfaction for the insult. We should learn from this that, no matter how small the irreverence offered to the Sacred Host in our eyes, it is a great offense in the eyes of God.[1]

O LOVE divine! Ah, why can I not love Thee better! O Jesus, reign in my heart, reign supreme by Thy love.

---

1. *Pelican,* Munich (1896). Maier, *Gedenkblaetter* (1890). *Tabernakelwacht* (Wuerzburg, 1900).

Prayer

O BREAD of angels, that has come down from Heaven, can I dare to bring Thee into my heart, which has been so often the abode of sin.

O Divine Lover, Who invitest us to Thy nuptials, and Who invitest us so lovingly, give the nuptial robe to this prodigal child who returns to Thee with all the sincerity of which he is capable. I confess before Heaven and earth that I am not worthy to be numbered among Thy servants, much less to eat at Thy table. Were I to receive my just desert I should feed on my tears for the remainder of my life, and be forever deprived of the communion of saints. But Lord, since Thou hast commanded me to approach Thy Holy Table, and hast threatened me with Thy anger if I do not eat of Thy Flesh and drink of Thy Blood, I will no longer hesitate between my unworthiness and Thy will; and I will draw near Thy table with confidence, since Thou invitest me with so much kindness.

O my Saviour, I cannot find in the Scriptures that Thou didst ever treat a sinner with unkindness. What more consoling than to read of Thy treatment of those proud Pharisees who were scandalized because Thou didst receive sinners into Thy company, and that Thou didst eat with them? Why, then, should I fear and draw back from the Holy Table?

It is true that I am a sinner, but I wish to sin no more: it is for that reason that I approach this divine Sacrament, knowing that it is from it that we derive all the graces which help us to overcome our temptations.

The demon wishes to intimidate me, but Thy word reassures me: *"Come to Me, all you who labor and are burdened, and I will comfort you!"* Since Thou invitest all without exception, and since I, more than anyone else, am tried by temptations, laden with iniquities, overwhelmed with misery, I will approach Thee with confidence, I will receive Thee with respect, I will embrace Thee with love, I will thank Thee with humility. I will go to Thy nuptials with joy, I will eat at Thy table with pleasure. I will serve Thee henceforth with more fidelity, and I will bless Thee in Heaven with Thine angels for all eternity. Amen.—*St. Alphonsus.*

Act of Contrition

O MY GOD I am heartily sorry for having offended Thee, because Thou art infinitely good and infinitely worthy of love, and because sin displeases Thee. I am firmly resolved, with the help of Thy grace, never to sin again.

Spiritual Communion

MY JESUS, I believe that Thou art present in the most Blessed Sacrament. I love Thee above all things, and I desire to receive Thee into my soul. Since I cannot now receive Thee sacramentally, come at least spiritually into my heart. I embrace Thee as if Thou wert already come, and unite myself wholly to Thee. Never permit me to be separated from Thee. Amen.

Anima Christi

SOUL OF CHRIST, be my sanctification;
Body of Christ, be my salvation;
Blood of Christ, fill all my veins;
Water of Christ's side, wash out my stains;

Passion of Christ, my comfort be;
O good Jesus, listen to me;
In Thy wounds I fain would hide;
Ne'er to be parted from Thy side;
Guard me should the foe assail me;
Call me when my life shall fail me;
Bid me come to Thee above,
With Thy Saints to sing Thy love,
World without end. Amen.

Ejaculations

O SACRED HEART of Jesus, mayest Thou be known, loved, and adored throughout all the world.

O Heart of my Redeemer, may the love of Thy friends supply all the injuries and neglects which Thou sustainest.

A Sacred Heart Reading

A FEW years ago, a loving mother, on bidding farewell to her son leaving for the African war, gave him a medal of the Sacred Heart of Jesus, making him promise to wear it always on his breast. Faithful to his word, the young officer never laid aside this pledge of his mother's tender affection and confidence, and to it he owed his life. In that glorious campaign, in which the French soldiers behaved so nobly, he was chosen by the commander-in-chief, as being one of the bravest and most valiant, for a perilous enterprise. Entering a dangerous ravine, the troops suffered greatly from the enemy's fire; the general ordered them to charge, and the young officer leading the way, they rushed on the Arabs who occupied the pass. His regiment was almost entirely annihilated, and he was himself hit several times; but the bullet which struck him in the chest, and would have caused his death, was flattened against the medal of the Sacred Heart of Jesus, and he escaped uninjured. Full of fervor and gratitude for so miraculous a protection, the young officer never ceased to proclaim the praises of the Sacred Heart, and to publish everywhere the wonders worked in his favor. Often has he been seen to kneel at the altar with his pious mother, to receive the Eucharistic God and to thank the God of victory for having preserved him from certain death, and restored him safely to his parental home.

MAY the Heart of Jesus in the Most Blessed Sacrament be praised, adored and loved with grateful affection, at every moment, in all the tabernacles of the world, even to the end of time! Amen.

READING 7

Story of the Blessed Sacrament
(Boxtel, Holland—1380)

At Boxtel, a small town in Holland, a blood-stained corporal and altar cloths are venerated by the faithful, on account of a miracle that took place in the church of St. Peter. A priest named Eloi Aecker, while visiting the above-named town, celebrated Holy Mass at the altar of the Magi Kings. He had the misfortune to upset the chalice after the Consecration. At the moment the Precious Blood was spilled the color of the wine, which was white and very clear, changed to spots of blood that stained the corporal and the altar cloths. The celebrant was entirely beside himself when he became convinced of the great prodigy, and from fear determined to keep the affair a secret. He took away the corporal and cloths, intending to wash and return them when the stains of blood had disappeared. To his surprise the water and the cleansing had no effect on the mysterious marks. After he had found his efforts fruitless at home, he went to a neighboring stream, a tributary to the river Fommel, thinking that by washing the linen in this running water he could succeed better; but all to no avail. Convinced of God's will, he decided to take the linens to the church at Boxtel and make the miracle known.

Historians do not agree regarding details of the event. Some say that a priest, doubting the Real Presence of Jesus in the Blessed Sacrament, was converted after seeing the miracle, but that he took the sacred linens home, washed them several times, and exposed them to the sun. Overcome with fear when the bloodstains did not disappear, they say he concealed the corporal and the cloths in his dwelling until the hour of his death, when he made a declaration of it in the presence of his confessor and two witnesses.

The news of this miracle spread far and

wide, bringing many pilgrims to this holy spot. It was one of the most frequented pilgrimages of Brabant, and in the language of the country was called "Holy Blood of Boxtel." God was pleased to confirm the prodigy by many other miracles. An ancient author relates that it became necessary to burn whole cartloads of crutches and bandages, because there was no longer room on the walls of the sanctuary to suspend these proofs of cures obtained through the Holy Blood. Even the stream in which the priest had washed the bloody linens became a source of heavenly blessings. By this means many were cured of sickness, and others were delivered from the powers of the evil spirit.

Pilgrimages to this hallowed spot continued for two centuries, but owing to the religious persecutions which later arose, the relics of Boxtel were at first carried secretly to Bois-le-Duc, then to the abbey of St. Michael at Anvers. The bishop of the diocese finally determined to designate a permanent spot where these precious relics of the miracle of 1380 should be preserved, and the collegiate church of Hoogstraten was chosen. Since May 20, 1652, therefore, the pilgrims came to that place by the thousands, especially on the feast of the Holy Trinity and during the octave, to venerate the corporal and the altar-cloths which have been stained with the Eucharistic Blood.

A correspondent from Hoogstraten writes the following: "Every year we celebrate an octave in honor of the miraculous Blood. On this occasion we expose on the main altar, in the transept of our magnificent church, three pictures that depict the miracle. In the middle we see the priest washing the stained linens, to the right the priest on his deathbed is shown revealing the miracle to the confessor, and to the left we notice the papal delegate with the bishop and theologians investigating the miracle. The relics, despite their five hundred years, are perfectly preserved, the spots being still visible, especially on the altar-cloth, which is of thicker material than the corporal."[1]

O MIRACLE of the wisdom and power of God! O Jesus, small in appearance as a lovely Infant, smaller still under the veils of the Most Holy Sacrament.

---

1. Wagenaar, *Church of Hoogstraten. Sentinel of the Blessed Sacrament,* vol. XVIII.

Prayer

I COME, O Lord, unto Thy sanctuary to
see the life and food of my soul. As I hope
in Thee, O Lord, inspire me with that confidence which brings me to Thy holy mountain. Permit me, Divine Jesus, to come closer
to Thee, that my whole soul may do homage to the greatness of Thy majesty; that my
heart, with its tenderest affections, may
acknowledge Thine infinite love; that my
memory may dwell on the admirable mysteries here renewed every day, and that the
sacrifice of my whole being may accompany
Thine. Alas, I am unworthy to join with Thy
minister in adoring Thee! I can neither feel
the extent of Thy blessings, nor acknowledge them as I ardently desire to do. But,
O Lord, be Thou with me, then, that by
Thee and with Thee, I may worthily assist
at this Holy Hour.

Glory be to God on high, and on earth
peace to men of good will. We praise Thee,
we bless Thee, we adore Thee, we glorify
Thee, we give Thee thanks for Thy great
glory.

O Lord God, heavenly King, God, the

Father Almighty! O Lord Jesus Christ, the only begotten Son! O Lord God, Lamb of God, Son of the Father, Who takest away the sins of the world, receive our prayers: Who sittest at the right hand of the Father, have mercy on us. For Thou art holy. Thou only art our Lord. Thou only, O Jesus Christ, together with the Holy Ghost, art most high in the glory of the Father. Amen. —*St. Clare.*

Act of Contrition

O MY GOD I am heartily sorry for having offended Thee, because Thou art infinitely good and infinitely worthy of love, and because sin displeases Thee. I am firmly resolved, with the help of Thy grace, never to sin again.

Spiritual Communion

MY JESUS, I believe that Thou art present in the most Blessed Sacrament. I love Thee above all things, and I desire to receive Thee into my soul. Since I cannot now receive Thee sacramentally, come at least spiritually into my heart. I embrace Thee as if Thou

wert already come, and unite myself wholly to Thee. Never permit me to be separated from Thee. Amen.

Anima Christi

SOUL OF CHRIST, be my sanctification;
Body of Christ, be my salvation;
Blood of Christ, fill all my veins;
Water of Christ's side, wash out my stains;
Passion of Christ, my comfort be;
O good Jesus, listen to me;
In Thy wounds I fain would hide;
Ne'er to be parted from Thy side;
Guard me should the foe assail me;
Call me when my life shall fail me;
Bid me come to Thee above,
With Thy Saints to sing Thy love,
World without end. Amen.

Ejaculations

JESUS, meek and humble of Heart, make my heart like unto Thine.

O sweetest Heart of Jesus, I implore that I may love Thee more and more.

A Sacred Heart Reading

A FEW years ago, as is related in the *Messenger of the Sacred Heart,* a poor woman who had scarcely ever known the blessing of health was at last obliged to keep to her bed, being reduced to a state of complete exhaustion. The doctor, thinking she was in a hopeless condition, did not prescribe any remedy; and being forced to send her children out to work every day, the poor widow was left almost entirely alone. She used to leave her door open from morning to night, so that the neighbors and charitable passers-by might come to her aid in case of need. Her patience was wonderful, and no one ever saw her yield to impatience or sadness. One thing, however, grieved her; it was the thought of dying without seeing the beautiful statue of the Sacred Heart which had been placed in the parish church. "Ah!" said she, "it is certain that I shall never be able to go to church again; I shall never see the Sacred Heart." Those about her replied: "Do not lose confidence; if it is necessary

you can be carried to church." The poor
woman began a novena to the Divine Heart
of Jesus, and asked to have a Mass said for
her on the *first Friday in the month of May,* at
the altar of the *Sacred Heart,* hoping to be able
by some means to assist at the Holy Sacrifice.
Her friends agreed to wrap her in a large
shawl and carry her to the church; but this
was not enough for her, she insisted on fasting so that she might go to Holy Communion. The first Friday in May came round,
and her daughter and a neighbor carried her
in their arms to church. After hearing Mass
and receiving Holy Communion, she heaved
a sigh and exclaimed: "I am cured! Return
thanks to the Sacred Heart." She rose up and
walked alone to the altar, which was decorated for the month of May, where for some
space of time she remained on her knees
praying; she then returned to her home
without support, and without experiencing
any inconvenience. Her cure was complete
and lasting; the poor woman restored to
health became the joy and happiness of her
little household, and she showed her gratitude towards the Divine Heart of Jesus by
never failing to communicate in thanksgiving, every first Friday of the month.

MAY the Heart of Jesus in the Most Blessed Sacrament be praised, adored and loved with grateful affection, at every moment, in all the tabernacles of the world, even to the end of time! Amen.

READING 8

Story of the Blessed Sacrament (Lucerne, Switzerland—1447)

IN the Canton of Lucerne in Switzerland, there stands a chapel which has been built for over four hundred years. To this very day the faithful make pilgrimages to the spot, the month of May bringing the greatest number of worshipers to the sacred shrine.

On the 23rd of May, 1447, a woman, led by the evil spirit, committed the sacrilege of stealing a consecrated Host from the tabernacle of the village church. She thought that by selling the Particle she might enrich herself, but scarcely had she left the church when she was unable to proceed any further, so heavy did the sacred burden become. To rid herself of It, she threw It into some bushes which grew nearby. The thought of the evil deed, however, haunted her so that she had no rest. Finally, responding to the grace of God, she confessed her sin and repented.

Soon after the above event, a shepherdess happened one day to be driving her flock to pasture. Suddenly the sheep refused to go further, and neither threats nor blandishments were of any avail. The young girl went at last and brought one of her neighbors to the scene, thinking that she could induce the sheep to proceed on their way. What was the surprise of both women when they saw the sheep kneeling in reverence before a certain bush, over which there rested a Host surrounded by a brilliant light, and having the appearance of a white rose divided into seven parts. The report of this miracle having spread throughout the surrounding country, the pastor of the parish organized a procession to carry back the Sacred Particle to the church from which It had been taken. But now a strange phenomenon occurred. Six of the different parts of the Host were taken and placed upon the paten, but when the priest extended his hand to place the seventh there also, to the astonishment of all It eluded his grasp and disappeared in the earth before the sight of the entire multitude.

From that time on the Almighty showered special favors on this spot by granting exceptional graces and curing different diseases. So great were the contributions of those who had been favored that the bishop was enabled to erect a spacious chapel on the spot in which were placed three large altars, the main altar resting where the bush had stood and where the Host disappeared.

When the building was completed the miraculous Host was placed in the tabernacle in a costly monstrance, where It reposed till the year 1550, when It was unfortunately taken by robbers who plundered the church. Even at the present day, a procession repairs to this shrine every year on the second Sunday of September. Many pilgrims visit the spot and, after commemorating the event, return to their homes healed in body and soul.[1]

EVERLASTING thanks be to Thee for Thy boundless love. Thou sayest, O Jesus, it is

---

1. *St. Benedict's Stimmen,* no. 12 (1881). Fleischlin, *Die Pfarrkirche zu Lucerne.*

Thy delight to dwell with us; it is also my delight to be with Thee.

Prayer

How many favors and mercies may I not hope to obtain from Thee, O my Jesus, hidden beneath the sacramental veils, at the moment Thou vouchsafest to come and dwell within me! How many favors may I not expect from Thine infinite goodness and power, in this most Holy Sacrament.

I hope, O my Jesus, that every Communion will sanctify my soul, cleanse it from every stain, deaden within me the fires of concupiscence, and fill it with all graces. I hope, O my Jesus, and on Thee do my hopes rest. I well know that I am absolutely unworthy of Thy mercies, I know that I have sinned many and many times; but I likewise know that Thou, my crucified Jesus, art my Saviour; I know that Thou art infinitely good and merciful, and in Thine infinite goodness and mercy I place all my hopes.—*St. Hilary.*

Act of Contrition

O MY GOD I am heartily sorry for having offended Thee, because Thou art infinitely good and infinitely worthy of love, and because sin displeases Thee. I am firmly resolved, with the help of Thy grace, never to sin again.

Spiritual Communion

M Y JESUS, I believe that Thou art present in the most Blessed Sacrament. I love Thee above all things, and I desire to receive Thee into my soul. Since I cannot now receive Thee sacramentally, come at least spiritually into my heart. I embrace Thee as if Thou wert already come, and unite myself wholly to Thee. Never permit me to be separated from Thee. Amen.

Anima Christi

SOUL OF CHRIST, be my sanctification;
Body of Christ, be my salvation;
Blood of Christ, fill all my veins;
Water of Christ's side, wash out my stains;

Passion of Christ, my comfort be;
O good Jesus, listen to me;
In Thy wounds I fain would hide;
Ne'er to be parted from Thy side;
Guard me should the foe assail me;
Call me when my life shall fail me;
Bid me come to Thee above,
With Thy Saints to sing Thy love,
World without end. Amen.

Ejaculations

SACRED Heart of Jesus, burning with love for us, make our hearts like unto Thine.

Our Lady of the Most Blessed Sacrament—Our Lady of the Sacred Heart! Mother and Model of all adorers of the Blessed Sacrament, pray for us who seek thy protection.

A Sacred Heart Reading

SOME years ago, a young man was unhappily led astray into the paths of Jewish infidelity.

Whilst still in the flower of youth, his heart was filled with dreams of glory to be attained as a distinguished musician. One evening he was asked to play the organ in one of the principal churches in Paris; there in that church God awaited him, and prepared for him, not a triumph of his self-love, but a humiliation a thousand times more glorious. Already the roof of the sacred edifice re-echoed the sound of the solemn chants, and the melodious tones of the organ had filled all hearts with recollection and prayer; every head was bowed and the God of the Eucharist had blessed His children prostrate in lowly adoration. The unbelieving musician, alone, dared to raise his haughty brow before that God despised by his forefathers, but it was in vain. A mysterious and invisible hand bowed his head and humbled him to the ground. A miracle of grace was effected, the young man was conquered; he knelt down a Jew, he rose up a Christian. His heart wounded by the Real Presence in the Sacred Host, he left the church; soon the waters of Baptism were poured upon him, and exchanging his fashionable attire for the coarse serge of a monk, he bade an eternal farewell to the pleasures of the world. A living example of the power of the Sacred Heart of Jesus in the Blessed Sacrament, he went from city to city, and from village to village, proclaiming the love of God, repeating again and again: "The days of grief are departed. I have found peace of heart since I have tasted the delights of the tabernacle of the Lord." If you would know the name of this privileged soul, ask it at the cloister of Mount Carmel, and they will tell you it was *Father Augustine of the Most Blessed Sacrament.* If one single visit to the God of the Eucharist transformed an obstinate Jew into a good Christian and holy monk, what may we not hope to obtain by devout visits to the Blessed Sacrament?

MAY the Heart of Jesus in the Most Blessed Sacrament be praised, adored and loved with grateful affection, at every moment, in all the tabernacles of the world, even to the end of time! Amen.

READING 9

Story of the Blessed Sacrament (Orthez, France—1845)

A MOST marvelous incident happened in the southern part of France in the year 1845. Among the Pyrenees there nestled in the pretty little valley of Orthez, in which, entirely separated from the world, is situated a monastery of the brotherhood of St. Francis. At the time of this incident, an irreligious movement was afoot, the instigators of which were the Calvinistic Huguenots. One evening about eight o'clock the good friars of the monastery were astonished to hear outside of the cloister walls the threatening cry: "Down with the Papists." The revolutionists, surrounding the quiet home of the friars, soon gained admission into the sacred precincts and lost no time in executing their work of devastation. Some of the holy men were killed by the sword; others met their death at the stake. But God is never conquered by the wickedness of men.

The prior still survived, and his one thought was to get the Blessed Sacrament to a place of safety. To his great distress, however, he fell into the hands of the mob while bearing away the precious Treasure. With fiendish delight, these wicked men tried to snatch the vessel from his hands, that they might defile and desecrate the Sacred Host. Neither threats nor force could wrest the holy cup from the clenched fingers of the prior, even when mortally wounded about the head and body, and when he died his lifeless hands still clung as fiercely as ever to their Treasure. Seeing that their efforts were in vain, they threw the body into the rapid-flowing Gavé, a stream skirting the monastery walls. But the noble defender of the Blessed Sacrament, though dead, still clasped the ciborium. Down the stream the corpse floated till it reached the city of Bayonne, and rested opposite the Minorites' Convent. Thousands hurried to the shore to witness the miraculous event, and a jubilant hymn of praise broke from the expectant multitude: "Praised and blessed be the Most Holy and Divine Sacrament."

A majestic procession was immediately formed from the doors of the grand cathedral, directed by the bishop in his robes of state. Church bells pealed forth their message of exultation; old and young, rich and poor, learned and ignorant, came to meet the Lord Jesus in the Blessed Sacrament.

On the arrival of the bishop and the clergy, the body of the murdered friar—still holding the ciborium—was pulled ashore. Without any effort the bishop took the holy vessel from the saintly hands, and amid the chanting of sacred canticles, the Blessed Sacrament was borne to the cathedral.

To this very day the ciborium is counted among the church's greatest treasures. The body of the courageous friar was entombed in the church of the Franciscans, where many favors have been granted to the believing suppliants.[1]

---

1. *Almanach du Tiers Ordre.* Jos. Soli, *Les Merveilles divines,* LII.

O MY JESUS I adore Thee in this Holy Sacrament, as my Lord and my God, as my Redeemer and Saviour.

Prayer

JESUS, *I return Thee thanks.* What other words can I say to Thee? My heart is crushed under its weight of gratitude, and it can find no words to express its thanksgiving. I owe Thee so much! All the canticles which will be repeated during eternity could not tell all I wish to say to Thee.

I will invite every creature to bless Thee, and I feel that the heavens and the earth cannot produce voices enough to express the transports of my soul, and to send up to Thee one act of thanksgiving such as I owe Thee. Dost Thou not give me in Holy Communion more than all creatures, more than the heavens, more than eternity, more than the angels, more than Mary herself? *He that is mighty hath done great things to me; and holy is His name!* Ah, couldst Thou do more? Thou hast given Thyself all to me—to me, so long Thine enemy, and who learned so

late to love Thee. Thou hast annihilated
Thyself to reach my heart, because Thou
didst behold it bathed in tears and thirsting
for Thy love. And Thou hast made this heart
Thy tabernacle and Thy heaven. O God,
give this weak creature at least the deep
silence of admiration; give me the humility
of the Seraphim; make my soul a furnace of
love. Let every pulsation of my heart, let
everything within me, let my whole being
cry out to Thee incessantly my love:
"Blessed art Thou, Lord, in the holy temple
of Thy glory, on the throne of Thy kingdom, bearing the scepter of Thy dignity.
Blessed art Thou in the firmament of
Heaven! O ye angels of the Lord, bless the
Lord! O ye heavens and earth and sea, bless
the Lord; praise and exalt Him above all
forever."

Virgin Mary, offer thy sublime thanksgiving to Jesus perpetually for me, who am
unable to express what I feel; offer thy
immense love for mine, that is so imperfect;
glorify for me Him whom I cannot sufficiently praise and bless.

Sweetest Virgin, O thou whom I have so
much happiness in calling *Mother!* O my
mild and too kind protectress, I pray thee

to teach me to love God as I desire to love Him. I give my life into thy hands; I consecrate to thee, I devote to thee, my heart; I beg thee to bless these prayers, which are far from expressing all I could wish to say of the most ineffable of Sacraments. Ah! it is because my heart is poor, because I am nothing but weak and helpless, it is because I have no words, but only tears, with which to speak of a Sacrament of which neither the heavens nor the earth, nor angels nor men, could speak worthily. Amen.—*St. Augustine.*

Act of Contrition

O MY GOD I am heartily sorry for having offended Thee, because Thou art infinitely good and infinitely worthy of love, and because sin displeases Thee. I am firmly resolved, with the help of Thy grace, never to sin again.

Spiritual Communion

M Y JESUS, I believe that Thou art present in the most Blessed Sacrament. I love Thee above all things, and I desire to receive Thee into my soul. Since I cannot now receive

Thee sacramentally, come at least spiritually into my heart. I embrace Thee as if Thou wert already come, and unite myself wholly to Thee. Never permit me to be separated from Thee. Amen.

Anima Christi

SOUL OF CHRIST, be my sanctification;
Body of Christ, be my salvation;
Blood of Christ, fill all my veins;
Water of Christ's side, wash out my stains;
Passion of Christ, my comfort be;
O good Jesus, listen to me;
In Thy wounds I fain would hide;
Ne'er to be parted from Thy side;
Guard me should the foe assail me;
Call me when my life shall fail me;
Bid me come to Thee above,
With Thy Saints to sing Thy love,
World without end. Amen.

Ejaculations

COME, let us adore Him and rejoice in Him, who is present in the Blessed Sacrament, whose name is wonderful on the earth.

Thou art hidden here. Oh, when shall I

see Thee revealed, that I may ever love Thee more and more.

A Sacred Heart Reading

IN an ecclesiastical seminary of the diocese of Rouen, one of the students was distinguished for his piety and brightness. The day after his first Holy Communion, he went to his director, to show him his resolution written on paper. "I am resolved," he stated, "to continue to wear the white necktie of my first Holy Communion, as long as I do not commit a grievous sin." The priest said to him: "I cannot take upon myself the responsibility of allowing you to keep so strange a resolution; you must go to your mother and ask her permission." This he did, and he was permitted to follow his pious wishes. George, for such was his name, with his resolution combined a rule for life to receive Holy Communion on the first Friday, and every Sunday and on the principal feasts of the year. In 1870 he finished his studies with the degree as Bachelor of Arts at the age of eighteen. When the war broke out between France and Germany, he obtained his father's permission to join the

Pontifical Zouaves under General Charette. He had been a model of every Christian virtue at college, and he was one also as a soldier. In the month of January, when near the town of LeMans, the Zouaves were ordered to go into action. George distinguished himself by his bravery and fell mortally wounded. At once he asked for the chaplain and said to him: "Father, three days ago I went to Confession and Holy Communion and I have nothing on my conscience; be so good then as to bring me the Holy Viaticum. I ask just a little favor; in my knapsack you will find a white necktie, and a rosary; kindly get them for me." When the priest returned, George said: "Put the white necktie around my neck." This the priest did, and having received the Viaticum, George added: "When I am dead, take off this necktie and send it to my mother; write to her and tell her for me, that this necktie of my first Communion has never been stained." Oh! how beautiful was such a death! Was it not the result of his frequent Communions?

MAY the Heart of Jesus in the Most Blessed Sacrament be praised, adored and loved with grateful affection, at every moment, in all the tabernacles of the world, even to the end of time! Amen.

READING 10

Story of the Blessed Sacrament (Turin, Italy—1453)

A PAMPHLET called "The Holy Miracles of the Blessed Sacrament," published in Paris in 1853, gives an account of the "Corpus Christi Chapel at Turin":

In the year 1453 civil war had broken out between the Savoyards and the Piedmontese on the boundary between France and Italy. The revolutionists in their fury wrought the complete devastation of the little town of Exelles in Piedmont, not even sparing the church with its sacred treasures. One of the revolutionists forced open the tabernacle, and claimed as his special booty the silver ciborium containing a consecrated Host. Together with the rest of the plunder, he placed it on a mule. Having succeeded in passing without mishap through several cities on his way homeward, he at length reached Turin, the capital of Piedmont. As he passed the Church of St. Sylvester his mule began to balk, and, in spite of all the prodding and whipping, the animal would not stir from the spot. Suddenly the trappings loosened, the bundle that contained the plunder opened, and, lo, the ciborium, surrounded by a heavenly brilliancy, rose in the air, to the amazement of the bystanders!

Great crowds came to witness the strange phenomenon, among others a certain Father Cicione. He straightway informed the bishop, Ludovico Rocagnons, who, with some of the clergy, immediately came to the place. Seeing the Host, which had now released Itself from the ciborium, he fell on his knees and adored his God. Gradually the sacred vessel lowered itself whilst the Host remained suspended in the air. Then the bishop sent for a chalice, which he raised on high, and the Sacred Species soon rested in the holy cup. A procession being formed, the miraculous Host was brought, amid prayers and hymns, to the cathedral, where It was afterwards venerated by the faithful.

To perpetuate this wonderful incident, a chapel was soon erected, called the "Corpus Domini Chapel." Mural paintings decorating the walls of the edifice give an account of the miracle. A Confraternity of Perpetual Adoration still atones for the insults and outrages our Divine Lord received in the Sacrament of His Love.

The present splendid church, erected in 1610 to replace the original chapel which stood on the spot, is the work of Ascanio Vittozzi.[1]

JESUS, my God, I adore Thee here present in the Sacrament of Thy Love.

Prayer

O HOLY of Holies, Who sanctifieth all things, I bless Thee, I glorify Thee! I adore Thee! May all Thy creatures bless Thee! May Thy angels and Saints bless Thee! May I bless Thee as they do during my whole life! May everything within me and without

---

1. L'Abbe Favre, *Le Ciel Ouvert* (Washbourne). Semeria, *Storia della Chiesa di Turino, Cath. Encyc.,* vol. XV, p. 93b.

adore Thee, O my salvation, my light and my love! May my eyes bless Thee, Thou Who hast created and formed them to contemplate the beauty of Thy countenance! O my comfort and my joy, may my ears bless Thee, Thou Who hast created and disposed them to hear the harmony of Thy voice. O sole object of my praises and my canticles, let my tongue bless and glorify Thee, Thou Who hast created it, and destined it to proclaim Thy wonders. O my life and my happiness, let my sinful soul bless Thee, Thou Who hast created it, and destined it to enjoy Thee for all eternity!—*St. Anselm.*

Act of Contrition

O MY GOD I am heartily sorry for having offended Thee, because Thou art infinitely good and infinitely worthy of love, and because sin displeases Thee. I am firmly resolved, with the help of Thy grace, never to sin again.

Spiritual Communion

MY JESUS, I believe that Thou art present in the most Blessed Sacrament. I love Thee

above all things, and I desire to receive Thee into my soul. Since I cannot now receive Thee sacramentally, come at least spiritually into my heart. I embrace Thee as if Thou wert already come, and unite myself wholly to Thee. Never permit me to be separated from Thee. Amen.

Anima Christi

SOUL OF CHRIST, be my sanctification;
Body of Christ, be my salvation;
Blood of Christ, fill all my veins;
Water of Christ's side, wash out my stains;
Passion of Christ, my comfort be;
O good Jesus, listen to me;
In Thy wounds I fain would hide;
Ne'er to be parted from Thy side;
Guard me should the foe assail me;
Call me when my life shall fail me;
Bid me come to Thee above,
With Thy Saints to sing Thy love,
World without end. Amen.

Ejaculations

W HO shall declare the power of the Lord? Who shall set forth all the wonders of His works?

Oh, how great is the debt of gratitude and love I owe Thee, O my Jesus.

A Sacred Heart Reading

D URING the reign of terror in 1794, the prisoners of the Commune, in Paris, in the dungeons of Mazas, were preparing to make the sacrifice of their lives to God. They ceased not to repeat again and again: "Come, Lord Jesus." And the answer was: "Yes, behold I come quickly." Suddenly the doors opened, the captives did not leave, but Jesus entered. A courageous woman, whose twofold character of American and Protestant enabled her to visit the prisoners without exciting suspicion, brought to the confessors of Christ a little box containing several consecrated Hosts, which a priest had secretly given her, begging her not to fail in placing it in the hands of the captives. The prisoners were filled with joy and consolation. "I am no longer alone," wrote one of them; "I have Our Lord as my guest in my little cell; I feel as I did on the day of my First Communion, and I shed tears of joy. O my God! how good Thou art! how true is that mercy of Thy Sacred Heart!" On the 24th of May, the hour sounded for leaving earth for Heaven; fortified with the Holy Viaticum and Jesus in their hearts, the saintly prisoners went forth to yield up their lives into the hands of God. A volley was heard, then one or two single shots; all was over, the victims were no longer victims but martyrs. Their grateful prayers were not offered in vain; the Protestant lady who had brought them the Sacred Hosts received in return, from the Heart of Jesus, the gift of the True Faith. She is now a Catholic. Happy woman who found thus a heavenly treasure in the midst of the horrors of a siege which destroyed so much earthly wealth! On her return to America, she was able to proclaim the gratitude of the French martyrs and the generosity of the Heart of Jesus.

MAY the Heart of Jesus in the Most Blessed Sacrament be praised, adored and loved with grateful affection, at every moment, in all the tabernacles of the world, even to the end of time! Amen.

READING 11

Story of the Blessed Sacrament (Avignon, France—1433)

LOUIS VIII, King of France, on the 14th of September, 1226, organized the Society of the Grey Penitents in order to atone for the heresy of the Albigenses. A large procession was formed and Bishop Peter van Corbie carried the Blessed Sacrament. King Louis was the first to show the good example in his beloved city of Avignon, for, dressed in sackcloth and with a heavy rope about his loins, he walked in the procession, accompanied by the Cardinal Legate and his entire court.

The Bishop carried the Most Holy Sacrament to a chapel which had been built in honor of the Holy Cross outside the wall and in this sanctuary the Most Holy Eucharist was exposed for public veneration. According to the custom of the times, a very thin veil covered the monstrance.

The good example set by the King in visiting Our Lord daily in the Sacrament of His love was soon imitated by his subjects, who robed themselves in grey sackcloth, thus organizing the Confraternity of Perpetual Adoration. So great was the zeal and the devotion of the people that the bishop continued the adoration during the night. It pleased God to make this sanctuary more famous by renewing in it the miracle of the Jordan and the Red Sea. For the space of three hundred years this devotion continued without any interruption.

The city of Avignon is situated on the river Rhone. The district around the city borders on the Durance and Vaucluse Rivers. As a result frequent floods inundate this part of the country, causing considerable damage and suffering. In the year 1433, the various streams, swollen by heavy rains, deluged the surrounding country. Every part of the city was submerged and on November 29th, the waters reached the chapel of the Grey Penitents, which was on the Dargue. As the water rose higher during the night, anxiety for the safety of the marble altar where the Blessed Sacrament was exposed filled the minds of all. Securing a rowboat, the Confraternity officials started for the church to save the Holy Eucharist. On their arrival they were greatly astonished to find that, though the water was four feet high along the walls of the edifice, it had parted by the middle aisle and left a perfectly dry passage. Still more wonderful was the fact that the space about the altar was not wet, the water seeming to have formed a perfect arch on both sides. Having made a short adoration in thanksgiving, the officials hurriedly left the chapel to summon their brethren to witness the wonderful intervention of Divine Providence.

The authentic account of this singular occurrence reads as follows:

"A wonderful miracle occurred in this chapel in the year 1433, as the waters of the flood reached the chapel. The flood was at its highest on Monday morning, the 29th of November. The water had reached the upper part of the altar, but though all the valuable papers and documents, books, vestments and linens were stored away under the altar, not one drop of water had touched them, everything being perfectly dry. On Wednesday the waters began to recede and by Thursday the people could again enter the church. Armand and Jean de Pussilliac, the wardens of the church, found that the water stood four feet high along the side of the building. The pews along the wall were water-soaked, whilst those in the front in the middle aisle were perfectly dry. No water had entered the room where the grey habits were stored away. Twelve witnesses were called and these called in twelve additional witnesses, three of whom were doctors of theology, and all averred that a stupendous miracle had taken place on the spot."

By the first of December, conditions having resumed their natural state, everybody had access to the church and bore testimony to the facts mentioned above. This miraculous event drew a greater number of pilgrims to the holy place. On the feast of St. Andrew, the anniversary of the miracle, a fitting celebration takes place every year, on which occasion the members of the Grey Penitents, putting off their shoes in the vestibule of the church, go on their knees to

receive Holy Communion at the altar
railing.

The church, though destroyed during the
Revolution, was soon rebuilt, and to this day
Perpetual Adoration is held there.[1]

O MYSTERY worthy of all adoration; O
Treasure of love, worthy of undying gratitude; oh, that men knew how to esteem Thy
gifts worthily.

Prayer

LORD, *give me this water,* the water Thou
didst offer the Samaritan woman! Ah, my
God, to me so cold sometimes at Holy Communion, even when I hold within me the
never-dying fire of the angels! To me so troubled by earthly cares, when I have in my heart
Him who is the eternal repose of Heaven.
To me so little deserving of Thy love, give,
oh, give me, my Lord, of this water.

Ah, my God, in my wandering days I
longed for everything but Thee. Incessantly
thirsting after some imaginary happiness, I

---

1. Duchesne, *Chr. Worship. Annalen des Hl. Sacramentes,*
Munich (1860). Ott, *Eucharisticum,* p. 256.

ran to every poisoned spring in the world, and my lips ever remained parched and burning, because my soul was void of Thy love. But since Thou hast now shown me the source of living water, which gives eternal life, give me to drink of it, my God, that I may no longer thirst. I desire nothing henceforth but Thee alone. River of love, inexhaustible source, where the elect and the angels drink, never enter my heart without leaving in it at least a few drops from the torrent of the happiness of Heaven.

When I consider my abjectness and my deep misery, I strike my breast, and am not astonished to meet some refusal, at least in appearance, in the midst of the infinite liberality of Thy love. Meanwhile, O my God, take pity on a soul that runs toward Thee, panting with desire, and asks Thee to give her a love that will prove itself by facts—a generous ardor that will follow Thee as a true disciple, as a child laden with Thy gifts, and who ought not to shrink from any sacrifice, and trial, and abnegation.

Give me, Lord, this love, this burning love! *Lord, give me this water!* Amen.—*St. Teresa.*

Act of Contrition

O MY GOD I am heartily sorry for having offended Thee, because Thou art infinitely good and infinitely worthy of love, and because sin displeases Thee. I am firmly resolved, with the help of Thy grace, never to sin again.

Spiritual Communion

MY JESUS, I believe that Thou art present in the most Blessed Sacrament. I love Thee above all things, and I desire to receive Thee into my soul. Since I cannot now receive Thee sacramentally, come at least spiritually into my heart. I embrace Thee as if Thou wert already come, and unite myself wholly to Thee. Never permit me to be separated from Thee. Amen.

Anima Christi

SOUL OF CHRIST, be my sanctification;
Body of Christ, be my salvation;
Blood of Christ, fill all my veins;
Water of Christ's side, wash out my stains;

Passion of Christ, my comfort be;
O good Jesus, listen to me;
In Thy wounds I fain would hide;
Ne'er to be parted from Thy side;
Guard me should the foe assail me;
Call me when my life shall fail me;
Bid me come to Thee above,
With Thy Saints to sing Thy love,
World without end. Amen.

Ejaculations

COME, O adorable Host, place Thyself on my heart as a divine seal which will make me known as the servant of the Most High, and will promote my admission into the heavenly kingdom.

Sweet heart of Mary, be my salvation!

A Sacred Heart Reading

WE read in the lives of the Saints that St. Alexis, who was born of noble and wealthy parents, renounced at an early age all the goods of this world and left his parental home to embrace the voluntary poverty of Jesus Christ. He had been rich—he became a beggar. At the expiration of a few years, he returned and knocked at the door of his father's home, asking for alms and shelter. His relations did not recognize him, want and privations having so changed his appearance that they took him for a stranger, and allowed him to take up his abode under the staircase of the castle, giving orders to a servant to take him daily a piece of bread and a glass of water. Many years passed by; Alexis saw his parents leave and enter the castle without knowing him, although he himself remembered them well. One day he fell seriously ill and sent to ask to see his mother. Just before breathing his last, he addressed her in these words: "Mother, I am Alexis, I am your child." When the poor mother recognized her son in the inanimate body of the beggar, who for thirty years had lived under the staircase of her palace, she threw herself on his neck, and embracing him, exclaimed, weeping: "O my child, my dear child, I recognize you, but too late!"

How many sinners after death, at the sight of Jesus, whom they have disowned, will cry out in like manner: "O my Saviour! O God of the Eucharist! I recognize Thee too late; I have passed thirty, forty years of my life close to Thy tabernacle, almost under the same roof with Thee, and I have not known Thee." What will Jesus answer? "And I also, I know you not." To deprive oneself of Our Lord in this life, and to be deprived of Him for all eternity, O God, how terrible a misfortune!

MAY the Heart of Jesus in the Most Blessed Sacrament be praised, adored and loved with grateful affection, at every moment, in all the tabernacles of the world, even to the end of time! Amen.

READING 12

Story of the Blessed Sacrament (Ammerschwil, Alsace—1832)

Ammerschwil in Alsace is a quiet little village loved by all the nearby inhabitants on account of the presence there of Mary's shrine, known under the title of "Our Lady of the Golden Sheaf." This humble home of our Blessed Lady became a popular sanctuary on account of a marvelous incident which happened there:

One morning a wretched man received Holy Communion in the chapel for the sole purpose of profaning the Sacred Host. Scarcely had he received the Bread of Life when he left the chapel and threw the Host into the grass outside. Instantly a stalk of wheat bearing three ears sprang up, and the

Sacred Host settled in the miraculous stem. A swarm of bees flew to the spot and wove a beautiful network around the Host, thus forming a waxen ostensorium, whilst angels' voices entranced those who witnessed the prodigy. The priest in charge of the sanctuary, having been summoned, carried the Sacred Host to its resting place in the tabernacle.

The pilgrimage of the shrine of "Our Lady of the Golden Sheaf" became one of the most celebrated in Alsace, until the invasion of the Swedes, in 1836, arrested its popularity for a time. The cruel marauders burned Mary's sanctuary, but strange to say, her statues— one made of composition, the other carved in wood—were found later, both uninjured, beneath the ruins. One statue still exists and is found in the chapel built in 1856 by Monsier du Lys, a canon of St. Dié. It was through the efforts of this holy priest that the Alsatian pilgrimage was happily revived. After his death the Capuchins of Colmar took charge of the sanctuary till the Revolution. Then the statue was transferred to the parish church for greater security, and the inhabitants of Ammerschwil bought the chapel, thus preserving it from destruction. After the Revo-

lution pious pilgrims sought out the venerated shrine, and soon "Our Lady of the
Golden Sheaf" beheld her children at her feet
once more.

Since 1842 the sanctuary has been cared
for by missionaries and each year at least
30,000 pilgrims visit the shrine.[1]

JESUS, my God, I adore Thee here present
in the Sacrament of Thy love.

Prayer

O JESUS, brilliant Star, who has taken
Thee from the firmament to plunge Thee
into my miserable heart? O Splendor of the
Father, who has covered Thee with such a
cloud? O King of stars, who has despoiled
Thee of Thy glory? It is Thy love that has
worked this wonder; it has placed a veil over
Thy face, as formerly over that of Moses, to
make Thee accessible to Thy feeble creatures.

O Sun of light, dispel my darkness! O
Sun of grace, take away my sins! O Sun of
love, inflame me with the fire of Thy char-

---

1. Fritsch, *Kirchen lexicon. Tabernakelwacht* (1897). *Les
Merveilles de Sainte Eucharistie* (1890). Monsier du Lys,
Memoirs.

ity! O Sun of justice, have mercy on me: make me just and innocent before Thine eyes. Alas! Behold me in the presence of the Sun, and yet plunged in darkness! Behold me in a furnace of love, and my heart colder than ice. Beautiful Sun, enlighten me; beautiful Sun, warm me; beautiful Sun, gladden me, console me, enliven me.

My God, everything in us ought to remain absorbed in Thy love when Thou hast entered into our souls. Our lives ought to be henceforth identified with Thine. It is no longer we who ought to live, but Thou alone in us.

Take pity then, my God, upon this inconceivable disposition of the heart of man to attach itself incessantly to trifles, to nothings, which partly paralyze the sublime effects which the august Sacrament of Thy love ought to produce in us. Do not cease, O my God, to enlighten, to warm, and to fertilize our souls with the burning fire of Thy charity. And when, after having come down from Heaven into our souls by Holy Communion, Thou returnest again from our hearts to Heaven, draw us entirely after Thee. Make our hearts follow Thee in Thy rapid course; and by the grace of Communion may we be brought, through our fidelity, to a heavenly life—even to the life of the angels. Amen.—*St. Augustine.*

Act of Contrition

O MY GOD I am heartily sorry for having offended Thee, because Thou art infinitely good and infinitely worthy of love, and because sin displeases Thee. I am firmly resolved, with the help of Thy grace, never to sin again.

Spiritual Communion

MY JESUS, I believe that Thou art present in the most Blessed Sacrament. I love Thee above all things, and I desire to receive Thee into my soul. Since I cannot now receive Thee sacramentally, come at least spiritually into my heart. I embrace Thee as if Thou wert already come, and unite myself wholly to Thee. Never permit me to be separated from Thee. Amen.

Anima Christi

SOUL OF CHRIST, be my sanctification;
Body of Christ, be my salvation;
Blood of Christ, fill all my veins;
Water of Christ's side, wash out my stains;
Passion of Christ, my comfort be;
O good Jesus, listen to me;
In Thy wounds I fain would hide;
Ne'er to be parted from Thy side;
Guard me should the foe assail me;
Call me when my life shall fail me;
Bid me come to Thee above,
With Thy Saints to sing Thy love,
World without end. Amen.

Ejaculations

WE adore Thee, O Most Blessed Lord, Jesus Christ, and we bless Thee, because by Thy holy Cross Thou hast redeemed the world.

Behold the Cross of the Lord; fly, ye hostile ranks; the lion of the tribe of Juda, the root of David, has conquered. Alleluia.

A Sacred Heart Reading

A POOR man asked alms of St. Paulinus, Bishop of Nola. The prelate, observing that one of the beggar's hands was withered, asked him the cause. "I am the son of a widow," he answered, in an agitated voice; "from my childhood I was disobedient to my kind mother, and, as I advanced in years, I ran through all her fortune. One day, when she refused to give me the last bit of money that was left her, urged by a diabolical frenzy, I struck her with this hand, which is now withered, and she fell dead. This dreadful crime took place on the night before Maundy Thursday, when I was preparing to receive my Easter Communion. Having hidden the bleeding corpse of my poor mother, I had the audacity to approach the Holy Table; but, O truly dreadful miracle! No sooner had I received the Sacred Host than my hand stiffened and, with the most terrible pains, became withered. My cries attracted the most astonished gaze of the whole congregation and, overwhelmed with confusion and shame, I fled, to escape being seen by those I knew. From that fatal day, I wander about here and there, bearing with me this withered hand, as the just punishment of my frightful sacrilege. Willingly would I bear this temporal punishment, if I had not to expect the still more fearful pains of Hell."

Touched by this recital, St. Paulinus said to him: "There is in the Heart of Jesus, whom you have so grievously offended, enough compassion and mercy to pardon you. Do penance, confess your sins with deep repentance, and then make a fervent Communion in reparation for your sacrilegious one." A ray of hope brightened up the countenance of the poor sinner, and he followed the advice of the holy Bishop; hardly had he received the Body of the Lord with all ardor and devotion when warmth and life returned to the withered hand; he was cured. O ineffable goodness of Jesus, who pardons every crime on true repentance!

MAY the Heart of Jesus in the Most Blessed Sacrament be praised, adored and loved with grateful affection, at every moment, in all the tabernacles of the world, even to the end of time! Amen.

READING 13

Story of the Blessed Sacrament (Seefeld, Tyrol—1384)

UPON the high plains of Tyrol, enclosed among wooded mountains, lies the village of Seefeld, belonging to the Cistercian Convent of Stamms, together with the parish church of St. Oswald and the chapel of the Precious Blood. This chapel is yearly visited by many pilgrims far and wide. The fame which is attached to this deeply secluded monastery arose from a miraculous occurrence which took place in the year 1384.

At that time, Oswald Mulser was Governor of Schlossberg, a fortress situated about a half a mile from the village. This noble man, swollen with pride because of his power and wealth, was possessed with the singular conceit of receiving Communion on Maundy Thursday with one of the large Hosts which are only used for the Holy Sacrifice of the Mass, that thereby his greatness and distinction might be advanced before the people. In vain did the priest object that at Holy Communion there could be no distinction of persons—that there high and low, rich and poor, are equal. Oswald Mulser insisted, and the priest at length, through fear and human respect, yielded.

Oswald, arrayed in all his knightly apparel, wearing his helmet on his head, knelt at the altar steps; but scarcely had the Sacred Host touched his tongue when the ground beneath him gave way. Perceiving that he was sinking he caught hold of the altar-rail, but it too yielded like wax. Terror seized the sinner, and in an agony of fear he implored the priest to remove the Blessed Sacrament from his mouth. The priest complied, and the ground became firm once more. Then Oswald, overwhelmed with the sense of his sin and the horror of his situation under the chastening hand of God, betook himself at once to the monastery at Stamms, confessed, and did penance for his pride. His wife, who had always encouraged him in his impiety, was occupied in tending her roses, which had unexpectedly withered, when word was brought her of what had happened to her husband. In her passionate pride she refused to give credit to the account, when lo! the withered bush revived, and three lovely roses bloomed thereon. But this miracle had not converted her; hardening her proud heart, she tore the roses from the bush, upon which she was immediately seized with madness. In her frenzy she rushed out into the forest, and, like a wild beast, fled hither and thither from tree to tree, till finally she sank down exhausted and died.

Oswald Mulser, having done penance, died, at the end of two years, a very holy death, and, according to his own desire, was buried under the doorway of the chapel of the Blessed Sacrament. To this day the deep impression of his hands and feet are to be seen in the church at Seefeld; the rich velvet mantle which he wore that Holy Thursday was made into a chasuble and given to the monastery at Stamms.

When the Sacred Host was removed from the lips of Mulser by the hands of the priest it appeared blood-red. It was preserved in the church at Seefeld, and, after two hundred years, was transferred to the chapel of the Precious Blood, which was erected by the pious Archduke Ferdinand, and there it remains until now, an object of the deepest veneration to the faithful, a witness to the Real Presence of Jesus Christ in the Blessed Sacrament and a warning to all who would dare to approach the Holy Table without humility, charity and due preparation.[1]

BLESSED art Thou, O Lord, in the holy temple of Thy glory, on the throne of Thy kingdom, bearing the scepter of Thy dignity.

Prayer

SACRAMENT of my God, my Jesus, my life and my love, how I love to be with Thee. Ah, how necessary art Thou to my heart! How sweet and tender are the sentiments Thou excitest in my soul! God of love, divine object of all earthly happiness, what peace I enjoy when near Thee! What

---

1. E. M. Shapcotte, *Eucharistic Hours. Cath. Encyc.*, vol. X, p. 114c. Pachinger, *Wallfahrts Medaillen der Tyrol* (Vienna, 1908).

holy joy, what transports even amidst the troubles and sorrows of my offenses. Before Thee the universe is in a profound silence! Before Thee all things are as nothing to me; Thou alone, O my Jesus, art all to me!

Ah, vanish from my memory all the masterpieces of art, the vain displays of magnificence, and human pride! I only wish and desire the masterpiece of the love of my God. O my Jesus, in Thee is every good, in Thee is all love. Great God, hear my prayers! Oh, that I could expire before Thy tabernacle, burning with love and bathed in my tears.—*St. Catherine of Genoa.*

Act of Contrition

O MY GOD I am heartily sorry for having offended Thee, because Thou art infinitely good and infinitely worthy of love, and because sin displeases Thee. I am firmly resolved, with the help of Thy grace, never to sin again.

Spiritual Communion

MY JESUS, I believe that Thou art present in the most Blessed Sacrament. I love Thee

above all things, and I desire to receive Thee into my soul. Since I cannot now receive Thee sacramentally, come at least spiritually into my heart. I embrace Thee as if Thou wert already come, and unite myself wholly to Thee. Never permit me to be separated from Thee. Amen.

Anima Christi

SOUL OF CHRIST, be my sanctification;
Body of Christ, be my salvation;
Blood of Christ, fill all my veins;
Water of Christ's side, wash out my stains;
Passion of Christ, my comfort be;
O good Jesus, listen to me;
In Thy wounds I fain would hide;
Ne'er to be parted from Thy side;
Guard me should the foe assail me;
Call me when my life shall fail me;
Bid me come to Thee above,
With Thy Saints to sing Thy love,
World without end. Amen.

Ejaculations

O MY HOLY JESUS, give me an upright and just heart, that I may love Thee, the

King of Jerusalem, and wait for Thy coming, and feed upon the Bread of God.

Jesus, teach me the hidden secrets of Thy
love.

A Sacred Heart Reading

ABBEVILLE, a small town in the northern
part of France, was visited one day by a
very pious priest who had been very much
devoted to the Sacred Heart. After spending
a few weeks in the town he was accosted
one morning by a somewhat elderly
woman to hear her confession. "I am unable to do so," he replied, "for I have not
the necessary faculties to hear confessions
in this diocese; besides, you have plenty of
confessors in the town." The woman
answered: "I will try and obtain for you
the necessary faculties; the salvation of my
soul is at stake."

These words made a deep impression on
the mind of the worthy priest, who agreed
to meet her in the course of a few days.
In the meantime he made inquiries about
the woman, and learned that for years she
had been very fervent and active in many
good works, but little by little she became

disgusted with her mode of living, had given up her pious practices, and, without as yet committing any serious faults, she was adding infidelity to infidelity: she was lukewarm.

On the day appointed the woman came to the priest and revealed the dangerous state of her conscience. The confessor, seeing in what a great peril her soul was, earnestly exhorted her to pray and spoke of the devotion to the Sacred Heart of Jesus. At these words the woman replied that she did not like novelties. The priest told her to be silent, and made her promise that for eight days she would reflect for five minutes on these two questions: "What has the Heart of Jesus done for me? and What have I done for It?" She made the promise and kept it. In a week's time the Heart of Jesus had transformed this lukewarm soul into one filled with energy and zeal, and she became the apostle of this devotion in that part of the country. After some years she died, leaving behind her a wonderful reputation for charity and devotedness to the Sacred Heart.

MAY the Heart of Jesus in the Most
Blessed Sacrament be praised, adored and
loved with grateful affection, at every
moment, in all the tabernacles of the world,
even to the end of time! Amen.

READING 14

Story of the Blessed Sacrament
(Ratisbon, Bavaria—1255)

IN THE history of "Our Saviour's Chapel," published in Regensburg (1859), the following account is given of its origin and the events that happened in the revered spot:

On Maundy Thursday, March 25, 1255, it happened that a priest was carrying the Blessed Sacrament to a sick person in Ratisbon. Across one of the streets he traversed flowed a little stream. A narrow plank served for a bridge, upon which no sooner had the priest set foot than he slipped, and the Hosts fell out of the ciborium into a puddle of dirty water. Only with great difficulty could the Sacred Hosts be gathered

121

up. The people, believing themselves guilty of disrespect to our Divine Lord in the Blessed Sacrament, on the very day resolved to build a chapel over the spot which had been consecrated by the touch of Our Lord's sacred Body. At once the work was begun, and the building was provisionally constructed of wood. By Easter the chapel was ready, and the Sacred Particles were placed therein. On the eighth of September it was consecrated by the bishop in honor of the Holy Saviour, and has ever since been called Our Saviour's Chapel.

Without delay the faithful crowded to offer homage and make supplication to the divine Saviour. Two years later, in 1257, a wonderful event which took place at the altar gave the sanction of Heaven to their faith and devotion.

A priest who was offering the Holy Sacrifice of the Mass in this chapel was tempted, during the Consecration and Elevation, to doubt the Real Presence of the Blood of Christ. At that moment the image on the crucifix, which stood before him on the altar, stretched out its arms, and took the chalice from his hands. Full of fear, the priest started back, repenting of his doubt, and then the hand of the Crucifix restored the chalice to him.

From this time the fame of the place spread far and wide, and the offerings of the faithful were so rich that three years later, in 1260, the magistrate of the city, by order of the bishop, was able to rebuild the wooden chapel in stone and to erect by its side a much larger church. In 1267, both chapel and church were given, as a donation, to the Order of the Augustinians, in whose hands the entire property remained until the year 1838. In 1838, on account of decay due to its great age, the church was pulled down and the chapel alone was left standing. As later on the chapel also seemed likely to fall, it was restored, and consecrated on the eighth of September, 1855. There is not an hour of the day when this church is not visited by devout worshipers who gather before the tabernacle and say their prayers with the greatest compunction of heart.

Beneath the altar, over which the miraculous crucifix, blackened by age, still stands, rest the remains of Brother Frederick, a monk of the Augustinian Order, renowned for his piety and simplicity. In fact, his life so much resembled that of the angels that God permitted the good Brother to be in constant communication with them. They often assisted him in attending the sick and even helped him to decorate the altars. Once in mid-winter they brought him fresh, blooming roses, which the holy man, in his religious simplicity, carried to his Superior. At another time he was very desirous of receiving Holy Communion, but it happened that it was his duty to gather kindling wood for the fire. Holy obedience obliged him to finish this work. God, however, rewarded the humble virtue of this servant. Whilst the Brother was engaged, the priest was distributing Holy Communion in the church. Suddenly a consecrated Host was taken from the priest's fingers by an unseen hand. On investigation he discovered that Brother Frederick had been given Communion by an angel. This remarkable incident happened in 1325, four years previous to his death.[1]

---

1. Gemeiner, *Nachrichten über die St. Salvador-Kapelle zu Regensburg.* Ott, *Euch.,* p. 211. Shapcotte, *Eucharistic Hours.*

O MY JESUS, in Thee is every good, in Thee is all love! Great God, hear my prayers. Oh, that I could expire before Thy tabernacle, burning with love and bathed in my tears.

Prayer

"MY son, give Me thy heart." Ah, how could I refuse it to Thee! To Thee, my Creator and my Father; to Thee, infinite greatness, and Who dost contract with me, poor, frail creature, so close an alliance that we are but two in one flesh, that I am united to Thee, body to body, soul to soul, spirit to spirit? So Thou didst say to us, O my God, to make us more fully comprehend this admirable union: "He who eateth Me abideth in Me, and I in him."

Oh, mystery of charity that astonishes the heavens and fills me with gratitude and love! Oh, ineffable union, real union, which makes the Christian a member of Jesus! O God, Thou dost deify my whole being! Let nothing human then remain in me; and after Thy heavenly and chaste embraces let my lips and my tongue, my heart and my soul, remain impregnant with Thy divine charity. May I breathe nothing but Heaven, may I no longer hunger for anything but Thee. Mayest Thou alone live in me, and may everything in me be given in exchange for Thine entire self, which Thou givest, O my God, in Thy Sacrament of Love.—*St. Alphonsus.*

Act of Contrition

O MY GOD I am heartily sorry for having offended Thee, because Thou art infinitely good and infinitely worthy of love, and because sin displeases Thee. I am firmly resolved, with the help of Thy grace, never to sin again.

Spiritual Communion

MY JESUS, I believe that Thou art present in the most Blessed Sacrament. I love Thee above all things, and I desire to receive Thee into my soul. Since I cannot now receive Thee sacramentally, come at least spiritually into my heart. I embrace Thee as if Thou wert already come, and unite myself wholly to Thee. Never permit me to be separated from Thee. Amen.

Anima Christi

SOUL OF CHRIST, be my sanctification;
Body of Christ, be my salvation;
Blood of Christ, fill all my veins;
Water of Christ's side, wash out my stains;
Passion of Christ, my comfort be;
O good Jesus, listen to me;
In Thy wounds I fain would hide;
Ne'er to be parted from Thy side;
Guard me should the foe assail me;
Call me when my life shall fail me;
Bid me come to Thee above,
With Thy Saints to sing Thy love,
World without end. Amen.

Ejaculations

JESUS, Son of David, have mercy on me!
O sweetest Heart of Jesus, I implore, that
I may love Thee more and more!

A Sacred Heart Reading

DURING the siege of Metz in 1870, a
brave captain of artillery was carried
wounded to the ambulance. "Surgeon," he

said, "do with me what you will, but save my life. I have a wife and children—I cannot, I will not die!" Alas, all was of no use, and it was necessary to prepare for that last great journey; but the poor man was obdurate and would not put his conscience in order. Who was there to have pity on his soul and save it from the eternal abyss? Another captain of artillery, a fervent Christian, determined to render him this important service. He put on his uniform as if to pay him a visit, and approaching the bed of the dying man, said to him with tears in his eyes: "Come, my dear fellow, a soldier ought to know how to die; give your poor wife and children the only comfort which is left to them, namely, that of knowing you died as a good Christian." He then insisted that the dying man should no longer put off his religious duties, and remained with him till the priest arrived to hear his confession. Reconciled to God and fortified with the Sacraments of the Church, the dying man exclaimed in the fullness of his joy: "I am happy, I am ready for the great review. I shall go up there unburdened and decorated; all is in order." He then kissed with a lively faith a medal of the Sacred Heart, which he had received at Rome from the hands of the sovereign Pontiff, saying: "I have never left off wearing this medal, Father; when I am dead, be so good as to send it to my wife; it will be my last remembrance, my last farewell." Thus was a sinner saved by a pious friend having pity on him and bringing him back to the fold of Christ. Oh, if we did but know the value of souls, if we did but know the desires of the Heart of Jesus!

MAY the Heart of Jesus in the Most Blessed Sacrament be praised, adored and loved with grateful affection, at every moment, in all the tabernacles of the world, even to the end of time! Amen.

READING 15

Story of the Blessed Sacrament (Bettbrunn, Bavaria—1125)

BETTBRUNN is a little village in Lower Bavaria, in the middle of which stands a little church, famed as a resort for pilgrimages. On this spot where the village now stands with its beautiful church, there existed in olden times only a single farm. The cowherd belonging to this farm was a very pious man, who had a wonderful devotion to the Blessed Sacrament. But he was unable to satisfy his devotion, as the parish church was more than five miles distant. In his simplicity he bethought himself to take away with him one of the Sacred Hosts, and at his Easter duty he carried out the idea. Having received Holy Communion, he secretly took the Host out of his mouth, wrapped It carefully in a cloth and carried It home, in order that, in summer, when he was accustomed to lead his cows for the entire day into the forest, he might give himself up to devotion; especially when in the heat of the day the cattle lay down under the oaks and the beechtrees. For this pious purpose the good man chose a stick, and in the upper end of it cut a round opening, in which he laid the Sacred Particle, and made It very secure to prevent It from falling out. This stick he always carried with him, and when the cattle rested he stuck it in the ground, prostrating himself before the Most Holy, and adoring the hidden Lord with profound veneration.

Now it came to pass one day that the cows, having strayed some distance, he desired to drive them back with his staff, but in his haste he took up the stick containing the Sacred Host and threw it after the cows. In this way the Blessed Sacrament fell out, and when he endeavored to pick It up, he found he could not do it. In his distress he revealed everything to the parish priest, who also tried to remove the Blessed Sacrament from the ground. The priest related this fact to Mgr. Hartwich, the Bishop of Ratisbon, who,

attended by his clergy, went to the place—
and after making a vow to build a chapel upon
the very spot, was able to remove the Blessed
Sacrament from the ground. The bishop
ordered a wooden chapel to be erected without delay, and after its completion the Sacred
Host was placed in the consecrated edifice.

After the news of this marvelous event
reached the ears of the people, the faithful
from all parts flocked together, and the number of pilgrims increased from year to year.
The priests of the neighboring parish were
put in charge of this newly erected home of
the hidden Lord. Very soon a village rose
up which received the name of Bettbrunn,
and the Sacred Particle remained until the year
1330, when the chapel was unfortunately
destroyed by fire, and so the Blessed Sacrament was lost. However, a picture of the
Saviour escaped destruction, and when a new
church was built upon the spot this picture
was placed in it for veneration. It is still in
existence, and remains to this day an object
of veneration to innumerable pilgrims who
visit Bettbrunn annually.[1]

---

1. Ott, *Eucharisticum,* p. 175. *Kalender für Katholische Chris-
ten,* 1865. Shapcotte, *Eucharistic Hours,* p. 90.

JESUS, Son of God, Splendor of the Father, Who veils His Majesty in this admirable Sacrament! Come, let us adore.

Prayer

AH! What can I desire on earth, what hope for in Heaven but Thee, my Jesus! Thou art the God of my heart, and the inheritance I desire for eternity.

O infinite God, God thrice blessed, Thou before whom the very angels are not sufficiently pure, what is man in Thy presence? Should he even dare to enter Thy temple, or address his prayers to Thee? It is true, my God; and yet, though I am a thousand times unworthy to enter into Thy temple, it pleases Thee to enter into my heart; it pleases Thee to unite Thy soul to my soul, to incorporate Thy Flesh with my flesh, to mingle Thy Blood with my blood, and to press, in the sweet embrace of a brother and a friend, Thy Heart, so holy, to my heart which is so miserable!

Ah! Sacred Heart, most loving Heart of my Jesus, repose often on the poor heart of Thy weak child; but first prepare Thyself, breathe into it Thy love, pour into it that lively faith, that firm hope, that ardent charity which ought to prepare the way for Thine adorable Heart; then come, O my God, O my Father, O the most generous of friends. Ah, come often, Thou whom I hope to love for all eternity! Come with every sun of this passing life, repose Thine adorable Heart upon mine. Amen.—*St. Francis de Sales.*

Act of Contrition

O MY GOD I am heartily sorry for having offended Thee, because Thou art infinitely good and infinitely worthy of love, and because sin displeases Thee. I am firmly resolved, with the help of Thy grace, never to sin again.

Spiritual Communion

MY JESUS, I believe that Thou art present in the most Blessed Sacrament. I love Thee above all things, and I desire to receive Thee into my soul. Since I cannot now receive Thee sacramentally, come at least spiritually into my heart. I embrace Thee as if Thou wert already come, and unite myself wholly to Thee. Never permit me to be separated from Thee. Amen.

Anima Christi

SOUL OF CHRIST, be my sanctification;
Body of Christ, be my salvation;
Blood of Christ, fill all my veins;
Water of Christ's side, wash out my stains;
Passion of Christ, my comfort be;
O good Jesus, listen to me;
In Thy wounds I fain would hide;
Ne'er to be parted from Thy side;
Guard me should the foe assail me;
Call me when my life shall fail me;
Bid me come to Thee above,
With Thy Saints to sing Thy love,
World without end. Amen.

Ejaculations

O MY GOD and Redeemer, can I contemplate Thee present in the Blessed Sacrament without being moved to a sincere and ardent love!

Thou dost give us Thy wonderful presence to console us in our afflictions, to save us from our sins, and to nourish our spiritual life.

A Sacred Heart Reading

PROVIDENCE has reserved for this century, which is one of material things and earthly interests, the example of a saint whose only thought was for Heaven, and who loved but the Heart of Jesus. To give an idea of the love of God with which Monsieur Vianney, the Curé of Ars, was animated, says his historian, it would be necessary to describe all the zeal, energy, gentleness and generosity of which a human soul, aided by grace, is capable. He thought and spoke unceasingly of the Sacred Heart of Jesus, and his words seemed flames of love. He continually preached on the devotion, recommended it to all those whom he directed, to the sick, to the afflicted, and to poor sinners. One day—it was the morning of the beautiful feast of the Sacred Heart— he said with tears in his eyes: "Let us all go to the Heart of Jesus, to the throne of divine goodness; there flows from It love and mercy sufficient to wash away all the sins of the world. Oh, if we knew how much this divine Heart loves us, we should die of joy! The only happiness on earth is to love

It, and to know that It loves us!"

After the example of this holy priest, of this indefatigable apostle, let us recommend and propagate the devotion to the Sacred Heart. "Let us diffuse in the world the sweet odor of the Heart of Jesus Christ," said the Blessed Margaret Mary, "and we shall be Its joy and crown."

MAY the Heart of Jesus in the Most Blessed Sacrament be praised, adored and loved with grateful affection, at every moment, in all the tabernacles of the world, even to the end of time! Amen.

READING 16

Story of the Blessed Sacrament
(Soissons, France—1115)

THE historians of the twelfth century
record quite a number of Eucharistic prodigies. The Venerable Guibert, Abbot of
Nogent, in his work *De pignoribus Sanctorum,*
relates this charming incident which occurred
in the city of Soissons in the year 1115:

On Easter Day a good and pious mother
had brought her young child to church that
it might receive Holy Communion, for it was
still the custom to give the Blessed Eucharist
to the little innocent children who were
brought by their parents to the Holy Sacrifice. The child, too young as yet to understand the holy ceremonies, gazed with
curiosity at the altar. Suddenly at the moment

of Consecration it exclaimed: "O Mother, see how beautiful is the little child the priest is holding in his hands!" Extending its tiny arms towards the sanctuary, it showed by its attitude that it was attracted by the uncommon vision. The mother saw nothing and wished to impose silence on the child, but it repeated its exclamations. Finally, when the priest placed the Host on the altar and covered it with the corporal, the child cried out again in a loud voice: "See, now he is hiding it!" This scene produced a profound impression upon the people. They at once concluded, adds the Venerable Abbot, that, to behold the wonders of God, childhood in its innocence has lights unknown to those who, advanced in years, are attached to earth and would judge all things by reason apart from faith.

A similar event took place, according to Robert de Mont, in a church of Angers in 1182. A little innocent, seeing a beautiful child in place of the Host, cried out to the congregation: "Come, see God!" But no one perceived the prodigy that it wished to show them.

The Chronicles of Vezelay and Tours, in the year of Our Lord 1116, recount the following supernatural incident: A priest was celebrating Mass at the abbey of Déols, in Berry, when suddenly the assistants beheld on the altar a little child standing before the chalice, in the place of the Host.

At Fecamp, in Normandy, a priest of great sanctity was celebrant of the solemn Mass of the day, being the anniversary of the dedication of the church of the Holy Trinity. At the moment of Holy Communion the Host in the hands of the priest suddenly changed into a beautiful child. He made a sign to the deacon to attract the bishops present at the solemnity, and by their order he transported the miraculous Host to a tabernacle where It was preserved for many years. This happened in the year 1182.[1]

O BLESSED Banquet, life-giving Sacrament, where the Christian truly eats Life itself! By this divine food I live in Thee, O Lord, and Thou livest in me.

---

1. *Chronicles of Vezelay and Tours* (1116). Guibert, *Chronicles of Nogent* (1115). Tresvaux, *Histoire du diocese d'Angers.* "Fecamp," *Cath. Encyc.,* vol. VII, p. 492d.

Prayer

YES, my God, Thou art my Life, and I now fully comprehend that to live far away from Thee is not to live at all, but sadly to pine and die. Thou art my Life! Thou Who hast so often united Thy Flesh to my flesh, Thy Blood to my blood. O admirable union! Divine union, which makes Thee live in me, and I in Thee! And if Thou art for me, if Thou art within me, what can I fear, O my God? Dost Thou not give to those who nourish themselves with Thee a peace, a resignation and entire abandonment of themselves to Thy love, which places them above the thousand afflictions of life?

Thou art my Life, O miraculous Bread, which was given to me by Thine angel, when exhausted with my journey through the vast solitude of the world, I went and threw myself at Thy feet, begging that peace might be restored to my heart. *"Arise and eat!"* And when I had partaken of this Bread come down from Heaven, my strength returned. Often nourished with this Bread of Angels, behold me wending my way toward Thy mountain, my soul filled with courage, overflowing with consolation and hope.

O God, how great are Thy mercies! How admirable are Thy ways! None but Thou could thus make man, surrounded as he is with all the miseries of a sensual and worldly life, an angel decked with every ornament of Heaven. Amen.—*St. Eusebius.*

Act of Contrition

O MY GOD I am heartily sorry for having offended Thee, because Thou art infinitely good and infinitely worthy of love, and because sin displeases Thee. I am firmly resolved, with the help of Thy grace, never to sin again.

Spiritual Communion

MY JESUS, I believe that Thou art present in the most Blessed Sacrament. I love Thee above all things, and I desire to receive Thee into my soul. Since I cannot now receive Thee sacramentally, come at least spiritually into my heart. I embrace Thee as if Thou wert already come, and unite myself wholly to Thee. Never permit me to be separated from Thee. Amen.

Anima Christi

SOUL OF CHRIST, be my sanctification;
Body of Christ, be my salvation;
Blood of Christ, fill all my veins;
Water of Christ's side, wash out my stains;
Passion of Christ, my comfort be;
O good Jesus, listen to me;
In Thy wounds I fain would hide;
Ne'er to be parted from Thy side;
Guard me should the foe assail me;
Call me when my life shall fail me;
Bid me come to Thee above,
With Thy Saints to sing Thy love,
World without end. Amen.

Ejaculations

O GOD, Who beneath this marvelous Sacrament hast left us a memorial of Thy Passion: grant us, we beseech Thee, so to venerate the sacred Mysteries of Thy Body and Blood, that we may ever feel within us the fruit of Thy Redemption, Who livest and reignest, world without end. Amen.

O meek Lamb, Victim of sin! May Thy
thorns penetrate my heart with fervent love,
that I may never cease to adore Thee as my
God and King.

A Sacred Heart Reading

FATHER Lacordaire, in a letter addressed
to a lady of the world, relates that a Polish
peasant was, at his death, condemned by the
justice of God to the flames of Purgatory.
His devoted wife ceased not to pray for the
repose of his soul; but thinking that her
prayers were not sufficiently powerful, she
wished to have recourse to the Sacred Heart
of Jesus, and have Mass celebrated for the
deliverance of his poor soul. Being poor and
not having wherewith to make the usual
offering, she went to a rich person, who was
an unbeliever, and humbly asked him to
help her; the gentleman felt compassion for
her and gave her some money. The holy
Mass was offered in the chapel of the Sacred
Heart, and with great fervor the wife
received Holy Communion for the same
intention. A few days after, God permitted
that the departed peasant should appear to
the rich man and say: "I thank you for the

alms you gave towards the offering of the Holy Sacrifice; this Mass has delivered my soul from Purgatory, where it was detained; and now in gratitude for your charity, I am sent by Our Lord to tell you that your death is near, and that you should be reconciled to God." The rich man profited by the warning, was converted and died shortly after, in the most edifying dispositions. Let us often recall the words of Holy Scripture: "It is a holy and wholesome thought to pray for the dead, that they may be loosed from their sins."

MAY the Heart of Jesus in the Most Blessed Sacrament be praised, adored and loved with grateful affection, at every moment, in all the tabernacles of the world, even to the end of time! Amen.

READING 17

Story of the Blessed Sacrament (Valencia, Spain—1875)

FOR A long time the parish priest of Moncada in Spain had celebrated Mass without any scruples of conscience, when suddenly he became the prey of a violent doubt as to whether he had been rightly ordained. It gradually became a real torture for him to say Mass. At the persuasion of a wise director he discontinued for a time his priestly duties. In his distress, to allay his doubts he determined to put his case before his bishop. He immediately set out on foot and journeyed to Valencia, the seat of the diocese. In this place it pleased Almighty God to deliver him from his trouble, and to give him light and peace by means of a very remarkable miracle.

Christmas bells were ringing forth their peals of joy to the starry night inviting the faithful to come and welcome the Babe of Bethlehem. The altar was all aglow with lights. The priest had been appointed to say the Mass. He had reached the awful moment of Consecration, and with trembling hands took the host and pronounced the words of transubstantiation with a quivering voice. As he raised the Sacred Host aloft, and knelt again in trembling adoration, the cry of a little five-year-old child rang out from the congregation: "O Mama, what a lovely child! See there, Mama! He is up on the altar." A little lad nearby, apparently forgetful of everything else, stood upon the chair and clapped his hands with joy. The boy's mother was embarrassed and bade him hush, for no one else had seen the vision of beauty; only the innocent child saw it when the Sacred Host was raised on high. Again and again he entreated his mother to look. "Such a beautiful child, Mama," he whispered, "just like the little baby over there in the crib."

The mother and child awaited to hear a second Mass which was said by the same priest at dawn, and again at the Elevation the little boy exclaimed, "Oh, there he is again, Mama, don't you see? The priest is holding him up in his hands and now he has laid him on the altar!" The mother bade the child be silent; she could not see anything, the great grace being granted only to her little son.

The priest completed the Christmas offering by saying the third Mass. At the Elevation the boy was all excitement, and the same scene was enacted as before. The happy mother repeated this strange occurrence to others, and through them it reached the ears of the priest himself, who it may be believed was greatly comforted thereby. However, his scruples were not entirely removed. He doubted whether the child might not have been deceived, and therefore he requested that the little boy be cross-examined by him. But the answers of the child were so accurate that he found no reason to doubt the reality of the manifestation.

Full of joy and filled with gratitude towards God, he invited the little boy and his mother to be present as often as possible at his Mass, and on each occasion the miracle was renewed. As doubts still lingered in his mind, he resolved to receive a final convincing proof. In order to obtain perfect rest he commanded the child to be brought the following festival to attend his Mass in the hope that the renewal of the manifestation might perfectly release him from his trouble. He bethought himself of a singular means. Taking three particles with him to the altar, he placed two upon the corporal and consecrated them, leaving the third one unconsecrated but within reach. After Holy Mass was ended he called the little boy to the altar, and asked him if he saw the Divine Infant in either of the particles, and, if so, in which. "Oh yes, Father," said the boy, "there He is! See, He is stretching out His hands." The little fellow seemed quite ravished with delight. On pointing to the other host the priest asked: "And what about it? Is the Divine Infant also in that other host?" The child answered, "No." "But are you sure?" queried the priest. "Oh yes, Father, there is nothing there."

At the last manifestation the peace of the good priest returned to him. Unrest and scruple vanished from his mind forever, and for the remainder of his life he served God with greater love and piety.[1]

---

1. Ott, *Eucharisticum,* p. 383. Shapcotte, *Eucharistic Hours,* p. 156.

HOLY Host, offered for the salvation of sinners, we adore Thee.

Prayer

IT belongs but to Thee, all-powerful God, to make the impious just, to raise the dead, and to change the hearts of sinners in such a manner that they are restored to their original purity. Let the hand of Thy mercy take from my heart everything that can render it unworthy to appear before Thine eyes, Thou whose purity is infinite. Heal me, Lord, and I shall be truly healed. Save me, O my God, and I shall be truly saved. Take from the soil of my heart all the briers and thorns that have been planted and nurtured there by my vices, and sow good seed in it instead.

O sole object of my love, He alone whom I desire! O Jesus, my Saviour, let me think of nothing save to love Thee, and praise Thee unceasingly, with all the strength of my soul. Engrave on my heart with Thine own finger the sweet remembrance of the innumerable benefits with which Thou hast loaded me; let me never forget Thy goodness! May I never again desire anything but to love and bless Thee, and may Thy holy and chaste love take entire possession of me. Amen.—*St. Augustine.*

Act of Contrition

O MY GOD I am heartily sorry for having offended Thee, because Thou art infinitely good and infinitely worthy of love, and because sin displeases Thee. I am firmly resolved, with the help of Thy grace, never to sin again.

Spiritual Communion

MY JESUS, I believe that Thou art present in the most Blessed Sacrament. I love Thee above all things, and I desire to receive Thee into my soul. Since I cannot now receive Thee sacramentally, come at least spiritually into my heart. I embrace Thee as if Thou wert already come, and unite myself wholly to Thee. Never permit me to be separated from Thee. Amen.

Anima Christi

SOUL OF CHRIST, be my sanctification;
Body of Christ, be my salvation;
Blood of Christ, fill all my veins;
Water of Christ's side, wash out my stains;
Passion of Christ, my comfort be;
O good Jesus, listen to me;
In Thy wounds I fain would hide;
Ne'er to be parted from Thy side;
Guard me should the foe assail me;
Call me when my life shall fail me;
Bid me come to Thee above,
With Thy Saints to sing Thy love,
World without end. Amen.

Ejaculation

SEE where Thy boundless love has reached, my loving Jesus! Thou of Thy Flesh and precious Blood hast made ready for me a banquet whereby to give me all Thyself. What drove Thee to this excessive love for me? Thy Heart, Thy loving Heart! O adorable Heart of Jesus, I am to learn to love that God who has given me such wondrous proofs of His great love.

A Sacred Heart Reading

IN the year 1821, a pious young woman in the city of Lyons* was moved with compassion on hearing of the sufferings and destitution of the French missionaries in heathen lands. One evening, whilst her companions were playing at cards, she was musing on the subject she had at heart, and she asked for the money won at the game to help the missionaries. Seated quietly by the fire, she wrote down in pencil on a card the simple and fruitful plan of the Propagation of the Faith, and little by little she induced the needle-women and servants of the town to join in her work. The first year she collected fifteen hundred francs; these details were given by the foundress herself. At the present time the subscriptions amount to five million francs, three million of which are collected in France. Brought in by so many hands, the weekly penny became like the grain of mustard seed, it grew and multiplied each day. On every side, men and women, rich and poor, great

*This woman was Ven. Pauline Jaricot. —*Publisher*, 1995.

and small, joined the association. If God
had said fifty years ago to that young girl,
as He did to Abraham, "Look at the
heavens and count the stars if thou canst;
the souls that will be saved by thy work
will exceed them in number," would not
her faith have been put to a severe test? Yet
today if still alive, she would not be able
to count the millions of souls saved by the
work that God inspired her to commence.
Oh, how the Heart of Jesus must rejoice
at this abundant harvest; how rich a reward
must He not reserve for the foundress and
associates of this fruitful organization! Let
us then love and spread this devotional
Catholic work, and we shall save those
souls for whom Jesus has shed His Blood.

MAY the Heart of Jesus in the Most
Blessed Sacrament be praised, adored and
loved with grateful affection, at every
moment, in all the tabernacles of the world,
even to the end of time! Amen.

READING 18

Story of the Blessed Sacrament (Naples, Italy—1772)

Sᴛ. ALPHONSUS in his book, *Visits to the Blessed Sacrament,* relates a most wonderful occurrence in connection with the Holy Eucharist. He obtained the full narration of the facts written by a priest who was one of the eyewitnesses of the miracle. He also states that he read the authentic process which was drawn up by the archiepiscopal court of Naples by order of His Eminence, Cardinal Sersale, the Archbishop of Naples.

On the morning of the twenty-eighth of January, 1772, at a place called St. Pietro-a-Paterno, in the diocese of Naples, the tabernacle of the parish church in which the Blessed Sacrament was reserved was found

155

open, and the two ciboriums, a large and a small one, containing many Sacred Particles, were missing. Search was made on all sides, but for a time nothing was heard about the robbers nor could any clue be obtained as to what they had done with the Sacred Hosts. At length, however, on Thursday the eighteenth of February, a certain youth, Giuseppe Crefici, saw a number of bright lights resembling stars as he was passing in the evening near the property of the Duke of Grottolle. The neighbors when they became aware of the prodigy were quite astonished and puzzled at the strange appearances. Night after night they were to be seen, and at last the conviction began to gain ground that these extraordinary lights might be a divine manifestation designating the secret spot of the missing Hosts. Accordingly a number of pious persons gathered together and made a most careful search in the neighborhood of the lights, but all in vain. Monday evening, the twenty-third of February, a great flame was seen moving around a heap of straw. With many others, the two brothers Giuseppe Crefici and Giovanni went there, and as Piccino, who was a companion of the others, approached the spot he fell suddenly upon his face; and after a few steps, Giuseppe felt himself pushed forward on the shoulders, and he also at once fell on the ground. In the same way and at the same moment the other two, Carlo Marrota and Giovanni, Giuseppe's brother, also fell, and all four felt their heads wounded, as if they had received a severe blow with a stick. With some difficulty the four got on their feet, and to their great amazement, beheld a light brilliant as the sun coming forth from beneath a poplar tree; and rising out of this light, to the height of about five feet, a dove fluttered in the air. Instead of rising higher, however, the dove, gliding down again to the earth at the foot of the poplar tree, disappeared, as did the light also. All the persons present gave evidence of this fact upon oath before the Vicar General of Naples.

Several persons at once went to work digging up the ground around the poplar tree, and at length one of the diggers came upon the Sacred Hosts buried some little depth in the earth. A priest who was with them placed the Hosts, some fifty in number, in a clean linen cloth, and amid general rejoicing carried them back to the tabernacle. It has been

confirmed that the Particles found on this spot
had not lost their whiteness, although they
had been buried for nearly a month.

On Tuesday evening lights again appeared
in the same field. From this the people concluded that they had not yet found all the
Hosts. Another search was made, but in
vain. Next night a quantity of tiny flames
appeared around the heap of straw. A careful
search was made at the exact spot, until on
raising a clod of earth a large quantity of
Particles was found lying underneath. The
parish priest, after being informed what had
happened, came quickly to the spot, where
he found everybody kneeling before the
hidden Treasure. The Sacred Particles were
placed in a chalice, and a table with a silk
covering was prepared. The Blessed Sacrament reposed on this improvised altar and
around it a number of persons knelt with
lighted torches, until many people with their
priests arrived from the surrounding vil-
lages. A procession was then formed, and
amid the blaze of tapers and the music of
sweet hymns the Blessed Sacrament was
carried triumphantly to the church of St.
Pietro-a-Paterno. As soon as they arrived at
the church, Benediction was given with the

chalice, amid the tears and cries of devotion of the people, thanking God who had by such wonderful signs given proof of His Real Presence in the Holy Eucharist.[1]

JESUS, my God, I adore Thee here present in the Sacrament of Thy love.

Prayer

O ISRAEL! O holy soul! How grand a thing is the house of God, the Church which possesses so august a Sacrament. O amiable Jesus! Thy beloved disciple may well say that it was particularly at the end of Thy life, when Thou didst institute this inestimable mystery, that Thou didst give to us the most precious pledge, the most signal token of Thy love! O incomprehensible goodness of God, to place it in our power to possess, whenever we wish, Him who ravishes the Angels, and who makes the happiness of all the Saints in Heaven! What more could we desire, Ah, why do not all Christians every day enjoy this great happi-

---

1. Vincent Giattini, *de Vita B. Alfonso* (Roma, 1835). Mueller, *The Blessed Eucharist—Our Greatest Treasure.*

ness, which God every day offers to us!
Amen.—*St. Teresa.*

Act of Contrition

O MY GOD I am heartily sorry for having
offended Thee, because Thou art infinitely
good and infinitely worthy of love, and
because sin displeases Thee. I am firmly
resolved, with the help of Thy grace, never
to sin again.

Spiritual Communion

MY JESUS, I believe that Thou art present
in the most Blessed Sacrament. I love Thee
above all things, and I desire to receive Thee
into my soul. Since I cannot now receive
Thee sacramentally, come at least spiritually
into my heart. I embrace Thee as if Thou
wert already come, and unite myself wholly
to Thee. Never permit me to be separated
from Thee. Amen.

Anima Christi

SOUL OF CHRIST, be my sanctification;
Body of Christ, be my salvation;

Blood of Christ, fill all my veins;
Water of Christ's side, wash out my stains;
Passion of Christ, my comfort be;
O good Jesus, listen to me;
In Thy wounds I fain would hide;
Ne'er to be parted from Thy side;
Guard me should the foe assail me;
Call me when my life shall fail me;
Bid me come to Thee above,
With Thy Saints to sing Thy love,
World without end. Amen.

Ejaculations

A SACRAMENT of Love art Thou, O most Holy Eucharist! Because only the love of our Saviour could be so inventive.

A pledge of love art Thou, O Most Holy Eucharist, which loudly proclaims and ratifies this love.

Holiest Jesus, my Saviour, I give Thee my heart.

A Sacred Heart Reading

DURING the fatal war of 1870 between France and Germany, a virtuous and only son, when on the point of starting to join

the army, placed himself under the powerful
protection of the Sacred Hearts of Jesus and
Mary. His good parents had also placed in
this twofold refuge their hopes for the
preservation of a child so dear, and whom
they looked up to as the stay and support
of their old age. As it always happens, these
hopes were not deceived. The young man,
a captain in the army of the Loire, encoun-
tered the greatest dangers, he was exposed
to the fire of the enemy's cannon and saw
blood flowing on every side, and yet he
received no wound. He devoted himself day
and night to nursing a soldier ill of small-
pox, and he was preserved from the con-
tagion. In a word, under every circumstance,
Jesus and His holy Mother watched over
this faithful servant with the tenderest care,
and he on his side, in the midst of the toils
and perils of war, never failed a single day
to recite his Rosary; and protected by the
Sacred Hearts he returned safe and well to
his family. To show their gratitude, the rela-
tives of the young man placed a slab of
white marble in the chapel of the Blessed
Virgin, bearing in golden letters this inscrip-
tion: "Gratitude to the Sacred Hearts of
Jesus and Mary, who have preserved and

restored a beloved son to his family during the war of 1870." Under every circumstance, in every danger let us invoke Jesus and Mary, let us take refuge in their hearts and we shall always be safe.

MAY the Heart of Jesus in the Most Blessed Sacrament be praised, adored and loved with grateful affection, at every moment, in all the tabernacles of the world, even to the end of time! Amen.

READING 19

Story of the Blessed Sacrament
(Petrossa, Spain—1559)

IN the life of St. Peter of Alcantara we read
that, from the moment he had celebrated his
first Mass, his union with God in daily
Communion through the continual contem-
plation of the bitter sufferings of our
Saviour took such possession of him that he
was almost constantly in the state of ecstasy.
No matter how much he endeavored to con-
ceal this great grace, he was frequently seen
by many uplifted in the air, held there by
some mysterious power.

The object of his love and devotion was
the Most Holy Eucharist, and this divine
Sacrament was the occasion of his most frequent ecstasies. When he approached the

sacred mysteries his heart was always con-
tented, because whatever difficulties otherwise beset him, then it rested in his Beloved.
The Saint on such occasions lost conscious-
ness of all things around him and prayed as
though no one but Jesus Christ and himself
existed in the world. On this account he
preferred to be close to the Most Adorable
Sacrament, and caused a little opening to be
made in his cell through which he could see
the high altar.

It pleased God to reward him for his
intense devotion to the Blessed Sacrament
by the following miracle:

In Petrosa, where the Saint had lived for
a time in a monastery, the feast of Easter was
to be celebrated with the greatest pomp and
splendor. The mayor of the town, therefore,
entreated the Saint to celebrate Mass out of
regard for the people, who came from all
parts of the surrounding country. The news
spread rapidly that Peter was to celebrate
High Mass. The crowd that gathered was so
great that the church proved too small for
the congregation, and an altar had to be
erected in the open air.

Satan, who had grown very jealous of the
Saint, resolved on this occasion to use every

means to distract the people in their prayers and devotion. Hardly had the choir begun to sing the *Credo* when a storm arose, threatening at every moment to destroy the altar. Although the people were alarmed, Father Peter remained calm and peaceful. In the midst of this commotion he sang the *Preface* and continued until he came to the *Memento,* which he offered to God with a gentle sigh. Thereupon a second storm arose, the thunder rolled on all sides and lightning zigzagged through the clouds, whilst floods of rain poured down upon the fields. The Saint quieted the people. Although the rain flooded the whole surrounding country, not a single drop fell upon the altar nor upon the faithful, neither did the wind extinguish any of the lighted candles. In fact, over the entire spot where they were assembled, it remained as quiet as the interior of a church. After the Holy Sacrifice was over a great song of thanksgiving rose to Heaven from the lips of the faithful for this fresh proof of the sanctity of the servant which God vouchsafed to display by this miracle.[1]

---

1. Ott, *Euch.,* p. 327. Paulo, *Vita, St. Petri* (XLC).

I WILL praise Thee, O Lord, with all my heart, I will proclaim all Thy wonders. I rejoice in Thee, O God Most High, and sing jubilee to Thy name.

Prayer

O MOST Sweet Jesus, infinite Goodness, who hast said: "If any man thirst, let him come to Me and drink"; I thirst for Thee; my heart sighs to possess Thee, and calls upon Thee with the greatest earnestness. Come, O cherished Spouse of my soul, and my only love. Come, and from Thy riches supply my extreme poverty. Delicious Manna, come to appease my hunger. Yea, I feel an irresistible desire to possess Thee, and I expect Thee with all the impatience of love.

Give Thyself to me, and it is enough; for without Thee all consolation is nothing to me, whilst with Thee, suffering is joy to me, temptation is triumph, and death is the entrance into eternal life. Amen.

—*St. Ephrem.*

Act of Contrition

O MY GOD I am heartily sorry for having offended Thee, because Thou art infinitely good and infinitely worthy of love, and because sin displeases Thee. I am firmly resolved, with the help of Thy grace, never to sin again.

Spiritual Communion

MY JESUS, I believe that Thou art present in the most Blessed Sacrament. I love Thee above all things, and I desire to receive Thee into my soul. Since I cannot now receive Thee sacramentally, come at least spiritually into my heart. I embrace Thee as if Thou wert already come, and unite myself wholly to Thee. Never permit me to be separated from Thee. Amen.

Anima Christi

SOUL OF CHRIST, be my sanctification;
Body of Christ, be my salvation;
Blood of Christ, fill all my veins;
Water of Christ's side, wash out my stains;

Passion of Christ, my comfort be;
O good Jesus, listen to me;
In Thy wounds I fain would hide;
Ne'er to be parted from Thy side;
Guard me should the foe assail me;
Call me when my life shall fail me;
Bid me come to Thee above,
With Thy Saints to sing Thy love,
World without end. Amen.

Ejaculations

SWEETEST Jesus, grant me an increase of faith, hope and charity, a contrite and humble heart.

Send forth Thy light and Thy truth; they have conducted me and brought me unto Thy holy hill, and into Thy tabernacles.

(*Psalm* 42).

A Sacred Heart Reading

A RELIGIOUS of the Order of St. Francis, named Alphonsus, had labored successfully in propagating the kingdom of God amongst the natives of India. To evangelize these poor souls sitting in the shadow of death was the object of his zeal and his preaching. After some years, he resolved to abandon his apostolic works and retire to a solitary place, that he might attend only to his personal sanctification. He wanted to become a hermit after such a strenuous life.

One day as he was kneeling before an image of the Sacred Heart, and praying with great fervor, he heard a mysterious voice which appeared to come from the Heart of Jesus, and which said to him: "Your prayers are pleasing to Me, Alphonsus; but your preachings and your apostolic journeys were still more pleasing in My sight, for they caused many to bless and honor My Father. There are in India thousands of souls who neither know nor invoke His holy Name: will you allow them to perish? And will you be indifferent to the glory of My Father, that glory which was the object of all My toils and sufferings?"

The religious replied, weeping: "Lord Jesus, I refuse not to labor; I will become again the apostle of Thy heavenly Father, and so long as I know there exists a corner of the earth where He is not known or loved, I shall never enjoy a moment's rest." He left his solitude and returned to India, where he honored God by the toils of his apostolate, and finally by the pains of martyrdom.

MAY the Heart of Jesus in the Most Blessed Sacrament be praised, adored and loved with grateful affection, at every moment, in all the tabernacles of the world, even to the end of time! Amen.

READING 20

Story of the Blessed Sacrament
(Dubna, Poland—1876)

A VERY remarkable event is recorded to have happened on the fifth of February, 1876, in a small town in Poland called Dubna, during the celebration of the Forty Hours' Devotion in the church of the Blessed Virgin Mary.

Amid the terrors of the revolution, the church of Dubna had been fortunate enough to escape molestation, and that reason, added to religious motives, contributed to make the number of religious worshipers thronging the edifice particularly large. As the Blessed Sacrament was exposed to the view of the multitude, soft brilliant rays of light began emanating from the monstrance, in plain sight of the people kneeling close to the sanctuary. Then a wonderful apparition took place. The figure of the Saviour appeared distinctly in the place of the Host, and remained there throughout the entire forty hours. Catholics and heretics, some from motives of strong faith, others out of mere curiosity, repaired to the church to witness the miracle, until persons in every walk of life and of every form of belief offered their solemn testimony as to the fact of the manifestation. This wide acknowledgment brought the affair to the ears of the city officials and as a result the parish priest was called upon to give testimony before the director of police. The Governor of Schitomar being informed, it was forbidden under pain of imprisonment to speak of the apparition. But the witnesses were not anxious to parade God's work before the incredulous, and consequently they were content that God saw fit to exhibit His marvelous power in their behalf. A written statement of the miracle having been submitted by the priest to the bishop of the diocese, the latter requested that the event should be kept secret, lest the church should be closed by the civil authorities.[1]

PRAISED be Jesus in the Adorable Sacrament of the Altar.

Prayer

I ADORE Thee in Thy Sacrament, O Jesus, eternal Love and Source of all graces, and I beseech Thee to cast a look of mercy upon Thy children prostrate before Thee. See, O Lord, how great is our poverty, and deign to help us.

Bless us in our thoughts, our sentiments, our words and actions. Bless us in our relations, in our labors, our trials, our sufferings. Grant by Thy grace that, doing what Thou requirest of us, we may become worthy to be the object of the blessings by which Thou wilt call Thy elect to the kingdom of Thy Father.—*Fenelon.*

---

1. *Annales du Saint Sacrament* (1880). Ott, *Euch.,* p. 717.

Act of Contrition

O MY GOD I am heartily sorry for having offended Thee, because Thou art infinitely good and infinitely worthy of love, and because sin displeases Thee. I am firmly resolved, with the help of Thy grace, never to sin again.

Spiritual Communion

MY JESUS, I believe that Thou art present in the most Blessed Sacrament. I love Thee above all things, and I desire to receive Thee into my soul. Since I cannot now receive Thee sacramentally, come at least spiritually into my heart. I embrace Thee as if Thou wert already come, and unite myself wholly to Thee. Never permit me to be separated from Thee. Amen.

Anima Christi

SOUL OF CHRIST, be my sanctification;
Body of Christ, be my salvation;
Blood of Christ, fill all my veins;
Water of Christ's side, wash out my stains;

Passion of Christ, my comfort be;
O good Jesus, listen to me;
In Thy wounds I fain would hide;
Ne'er to be parted from Thy side;
Guard me should the foe assail me;
Call me when my life shall fail me;
Bid me come to Thee above,
With Thy Saints to sing Thy love,
World without end. Amen.

Ejaculations

JESUS, my God, I love Thee above all things.

O Jesus, living in Mary, come and live in Thy servants, in the spirit of Thy holiness, in the fullness of Thy power, in the truth of Thy virtues, in the perfection of Thy ways, in the communion of Thy mysteries; subdue every hostile power, in Thy spirit, for the glory of the Father.

A Sacred Heart Reading

A PRIEST relates the following conversion of a great sinner, in which the goodness of the Heart of Jesus is strikingly manifested: "A young man, one of my parishioners, whose parents had given up their practice of religion, became so impious and lawless that he scandalized even those who led bad lives. The excesses in which he indulged brought on an affection of the lungs which, gradually developing, was slowly leading him to the grave. I visited him and gave him many proofs of the interest I took in him; but he met all my advances with blasphemies and insults, even refusing to say a 'Hail Mary.' His state filled me with grief. 'My good friend,' said I to one of my curates, 'go at once to Paray-le-Monial; ask prayers for our poor dying man, and place his name in the Heart of Jesus.' He set off without delay, and the next day he was at Paray-le-Monial with the pilgrims from Dijon. Prayers were said and Communions offered for the lost sheep, and his name was placed in a silver heart near the altar of the Heart of Jesus. Full of hope we went again to visit the sick man. 'I prayed for you at Paray,' said the curate, 'and I have brought you a medal of the Sacred Heart.' 'I thank you,' replied the dying sinner, and calling his mother he asked for a ribbon, to which he attached the medal, placed it round his neck, and even kissed it with respect. 'Now,' said he, 'I wish to go to confession, and it must be this very day.' He received all the Sacraments of the Church, to the great edification of all present. Whilst I administered Extreme Unction, he said: 'Do not hurry, Father, I must follow what you say, and ask pardon for my sins. Oh, how good is the Heart of Jesus in waiting for and pardoning me; if I could live longer, how much I would love It.' He died the following day, blessing the Heart of Jesus."

MAY the Heart of Jesus in the Most Blessed Sacrament be praised, adored and loved with grateful affection, at every moment, in all the tabernacles of the world, even to the end of time! Amen.

READING 21

Story of the Blessed Sacrament (Bordeaux, France—1865)

O N a certain Thursday in the month of May, 1865, in a convent chapel of the Sisters of St. Joseph in the city of Bordeaux, France, our Blessed Lord appeared in visible form during Benediction of the Most Blessed Sacrament to the assembled worshipers.

The Sisters of St. Joseph and their pupils had gathered in the chapel, as was their custom on Thursday evenings, to assist at Exposition of the Blessed Sacrament, followed by Benediction. The aged priest conducting the services was kneeling very devoutly at the foot of the altar, whilst the choir was singing the *Pange Lingua,* when suddenly the acolyte noticed a mysterious change about the monstrance. Going over to the priest, he said in a trembling voice: "Father, I think Our Lord is appearing." Raising his eyes, the holy man gazed in astonishment at the miracle, yet he doubted lest it might be an illusion caused by the reflection of the gas jet. Soon, however, his misgivings vanished, and with trembling awe the servant of God prostrated himself before the altar. At the same time two little girls, who had recently received their first Holy Communion, were praying most fervently nearby, when suddenly they beheld the radiant face of the God-Man, Jesus Christ, in the Blessed Sacrament. Whispering to their companions the magic words: "Look! Our Lord is appearing!" the news soon spread through the chapel and all in humble adoration rendered homage to their Saviour.

The priest himself stated that at the moment of Benediction he beheld the face of our Divine Lord gleaming with heavenly beauty —His sacred head wearing a tonsure as is the custom of priests in France. The apparition continued till after Benediction had been given, when the Host again resumed its former appearance. Untold joy, astonishment and adoration filled the hearts of the happy witnesses of the miracle. Cardinal Donnet,

Archbishop of Bordeaux, was notified, but he gave strict orders that the occurrence should be kept a secret. On Thursday following, our Divine Lord rewarded the obedience of the Sisters by a repetition of the same miraculous appearance, which event induced the Archbishop to establish a special memorial feast for the convent.[1]

Hail, O Jesus, my Redeemer, in the Blessed Sacrament.

Prayer

Show Thyself to me, O my Consoler! Let me see Thee, Who art the Light of my eyes! Come, O joy of my spirit! Let me see Thee, O joy of my heart! Let me love Thee, O Life of my soul! Appear to my eyes, Thou Who art my dearest delight and my sweetest consolation! O Lord, my God, Thou art my Life and the only glory of my soul. Let me find Thee, Whom my heart desires; let me possess Thee, O Love of my soul! Ah, that it were granted me to clasp Thee in my

---

1. *Annales du Saint Sacrament* (1865). Ott, *Eucharisticum*, p. 716.

arms, Divine Jesus, the possession of Whom
excites in me such lively transports of joy!
May I enjoy Thee, Eternal Beatitude! May
I enjoy Thee with all my heart, Who art the
supreme Love of my soul! Let me love Thee,
O Lord, Who art my strength, my support,
my refuge and my Saviour.

O Spirit of life, Who vivifiest all things!
O Life of my life! O Life through Whom
I live again, and without Whom I am lost!
O Life through Whom I find joy, and without Whom affliction is my lot! O Life, source
of life—O Life so sweet and so amiable that
we cannot forget Thee, where art Thou?
Where shall I find Thee? For I wish to resign
my existence, to live only in Thee. Come to
my soul, come to my heart, abandon Thyself
to my senses, be ready to come to my aid.

Alas, I am languishing from love! I am
dying without Thee, and it is only by thinking of Thee that I am born again to life! Thy
heavenly perfumes recall me to life, the
remembrance of Thee restores me to vigor,
and the sight of Thy glory alone satiates me.
O Life of my soul! Ah, my poor soul sighs
after the possession of Thee; she loses her
strength and faints away when thinking of
Thee. Amen.—*St. Augustine.*

Act of Contrition

O MY GOD I am heartily sorry for having offended Thee, because Thou art infinitely good and infinitely worthy of love, and because sin displeases Thee. I am firmly resolved, with the help of Thy grace, never to sin again.

Spiritual Communion

MY JESUS, I believe that Thou art present in the most Blessed Sacrament. I love Thee above all things, and I desire to receive Thee into my soul. Since I cannot now receive Thee sacramentally, come at least spiritually into my heart. I embrace Thee as if Thou wert already come, and unite myself wholly to Thee. Never permit me to be separated from Thee. Amen.

Anima Christi

SOUL OF CHRIST, be my sanctification;
Body of Christ, be my salvation;
Blood of Christ, fill all my veins;
Water of Christ's side, wash out my stains;

Passion of Christ, my comfort be;
O good Jesus, listen to me;
In Thy wounds I fain would hide;
Ne'er to be parted from Thy side;
Guard me should the foe assail me;
Call me when my life shall fail me;
Bid me come to Thee above,
With Thy Saints to sing Thy love,
World without end. Amen.

Ejaculations

MY Jesus, mercy.

My sweetest Jesus, be not my judge, but my Saviour.

A Sacred Heart Reading

A PIOUS and devoted mother was at the point of death; her cure was hopeless unless she submitted to a painful operation. Wishing to live for her son's sake, but above all to secure the salvation of her only child, the courageous woman placed herself in the hands of the doctors. Her son was present, in compliance with his mother's wishes, to witness the operation. She underwent the terrible ordeal without any opiates. The terrible operation began; not even a sigh was heard, nor did a cry escape her; but just at the finish when the sharp edge of the knife approached too near the heart the poor woman moved slightly, and gently murmured: "O my God!" It was then that the son, in a frenzy of grief, at the sight of the lacerated breast uttered a blasphemous imprecation. "My son," said his mother, "be silent; you give me more pain than the operators, for you insult Him who strengthens and consoles me," and opening her hand she showed him a small crucifix she held, to which she owed the courage she had shown.

After several months of great suffering, this heroic woman died, blessing her son, and saying to him: "Keep my cross, it has given me such consolation." The crucifix has ever been preserved in the family, and it became for her son the most precious remembrance of his pious mother. Christians, afflicted souls, preserve the cross of the Heart of Jesus, and it will comfort you and save you.

MAY the Heart of Jesus in the Most Blessed Sacrament be praised, adored and loved with grateful affection, at every moment, in all the tabernacles of the world, even to the end of time! Amen.

READING 22

Story of the Blessed Sacrament
(Assisi, Italy; 1649)

IN the year 1649 John Frederick, Duke of
Brunswick, then about twenty-five years
old, undertook a journey through Europe to
visit the various courts, and among others
he visited Rome. Though not a Catholic the
duke was greatly edified by all he saw in the
Papal City. During his stay he was anxious
to go to Assisi, in order to become ac-
quainted with the saint whose holiness was
renowned even in the duke's own country.
Pope Innocent, therefore, gave him a letter
of introduction to the convent, asking the
Fathers' permission for an interview with
Joseph of Cupertino, in the hopes of the
duke's final conversion. The superior has-

tened to comply with the request, receiving the prince and his royal friends with honor. At once the duke requested to see Father Joseph. The following day being Sunday, the prince and two counts, one of whom was a Protestant and the other a Catholic, were taken secretly to the chapel where the Saint usually said Mass. No one was aware of this, and Joseph did not know of the arrival of the strangers. He was standing at the altar, in the act of breaking the Host, as the duke and his friends entered the chapel. Suddenly a deep sigh escaped the lips of the Saint, and laying the Host down upon the paten he fell into an ecstasy.

The duke, being much moved by this strange sight, requested the superior after Mass to inquire of Joseph what that strange cry and sigh meant. The superior replied that the Saint was not always willing to give such explanations, but at the request of the duke he would require it from him under obedience. The Saint, when placed under this obedience, replied: "Ah, the strangers whom thou didst send to hear my Mass are of a hard heart and do not believe all that the Catholic Church teaches. On this account the Lamb became hard in my hands this morning, and I could not break It." The young duke, struck at this reply, desired after dinner to converse with the Saint. The conversation lasted until evening.

The following morning the duke attended the Saint's Mass. A new miracle awaited his eyes. At the moment of the elevation there appeared upon the Host the form of a black cross, and at the same time, uttering the same strange cry, Joseph was raised high in the air and remained so for a short space of time. Then the duke cried out: "Accursed be the day that I came into this country! In my own land I was at peace, but here I have found only anguish and distress of conscience." The other prince, however, began to weep at the miracle, for a ray of truth had touched him, and his heart was softened, although he still withstood the call of God. Joseph, enlightened by the grace of God, perceived the strife which was going on in his soul, and smiling at his irresolution, said to a friend after Mass, "Let us rejoice; the deer is wounded."

After Holy Mass the duke conversed with Joseph until midday. After dinner he desired to return to the cell of the Saint, but Joseph met him and said: "Go, pray at the altar of St. Francis, attend Compline and the procession, and do all that thou seest the brethren do." The duke, entirely humbled, obeyed the Saint and followed instructions as he was told. Accompanied by Cardinals Frachiette and Rapachicioli he threw himself before the Blessed Sacrament, and said with a loud voice: "The King of the whole world is adored in this church. I believe and acknowledge all the Catholic Church acknowledges and believes." Once more a wandering child was won to the arms of Mother Church. During the remainder of that day and also to a late hour that night the duke conversed with the Saint, learning the mysteries of Faith. The next day he resumed his journey to his own country, promising, however, to return the following year and make public reparation for his errors. And the prince kept his word.[1]

BEHOLD all the Angels serve Thee in Thy temple day and night: they stand before Thee, they fall on their faces and adore Thee, O God, Who livest forever.

---

1. Huguet, *Andacht zur Hl. Eucharistie.* Stadler, *Heiligen Lexicon. Life of Joseph Cupertino* (Aachen, 1843).

Prayer

MY Lord and my God, I believe that Thou art present, though hidden under the sacramental veil; I renounce my own judgment and the testimony of my own senses; Thou art my God and my Saviour! Alas, what have I done? I have sinned against Thee, my Lord and my God. I am unworthy to approach Thee. O divine Lamb, that takest away the sins of the world, I conjure Thee by Thy Sacred Wounds, the only refuge of the sinner, to grant me mercy. My Lord and my God, grant that I may repeat these sweet words during my life and at the hour of my death, and in the unfading glory of eternity. My Lord and my God, dart forth from Thy Sacred Wounds a ray of light and love, to penetrate and pierce my heart even to its inmost recesses. Enlighten my mind, inflame my will, that all the powers and affections of my soul may be consecrated with an eternal devotion to Thee, my Lord and my God.

—St. Bonaventure.

Act of Contrition

O MY GOD I am heartily sorry for having offended Thee, because Thou art infinitely good and infinitely worthy of love, and because sin displeases Thee. I am firmly resolved, with the help of Thy grace, never to sin again.

Spiritual Communion

MY JESUS, I believe that Thou art present in the most Blessed Sacrament. I love Thee above all things, and I desire to receive Thee into my soul. Since I cannot now receive Thee sacramentally, come at least spiritually into my heart. I embrace Thee as if Thou wert already come, and unite myself wholly to Thee. Never permit me to be separated from Thee. Amen.

Anima Christi

SOUL OF CHRIST, be my sanctification;
Body of Christ, be my salvation;
Blood of Christ, fill all my veins;
Water of Christ's side, wash out my stains;

Passion of Christ, my comfort be;
O good Jesus, listen to me;
In Thy wounds I fain would hide;
Ne'er to be parted from Thy side;
Guard me should the foe assail me;
Call me when my life shall fail me;
Bid me come to Thee above,
With Thy Saints to sing Thy love,
World without end. Amen.

Ejaculations

SAVIOUR of the world, have mercy on us.
Jesus, spotless Sacrifice, we adore Thee.

A Sacred Heart Reading

ON the Feast of the Assumption, many
hundred years ago, a celebrated queen said
to her two daughters: "Put on your most
beautiful dresses and your crowns of gold,
and let us go down together to the town and
hear Mass at the church of Our Lady." The
two princesses dressed themselves as their
mother had ordered, and entering the
church they knelt down opposite the
crucifix.

At the sight of the figure of her Saviour,

naked, bleeding and dying, the younger princess took off her crown and all her ornaments and prostrated herself on the pavement of the church. Her mother, surprised at her conduct, was about to express her disapproval when the young girl, with touching accent, addressed her thus: "Behold before my eyes my King and my God, the sweet and merciful Jesus, who is crowned with sharp thorns, naked and bleeding, and shall I, a wretched sinner, remain before Him wearing a crown of gold and precious stones?" And she wept bitterly; for the love of the Heart of Jesus had already wounded her tender heart.

The young princess grew up choosing always the crown of thorns offered by Jesus in preference to that of gold held out by the world, and in after life she became St. Elizabeth, Queen of Hungary. Learn from this story, O Christians, that in order to deserve the crown of glory in Heaven, you must here on earth wear the crown of thorns; the one must precede the other.

MAY the Heart of Jesus in the Most Blessed Sacrament be praised, adored and loved with grateful affection, at every moment, in all the tabernacles of the world, even to the end of time! Amen.

READING 23

Story of the Blessed Sacrament (Vierge-aux-Boise, France—1859)

AN extraordinary circumstance occurred to the Reverend pastor of Vierge-aux-Boise on February 7th, 1859, in a church in France. It took place whilst he was saying Mass.

During the Holy Sacrifice, after the Consecration, a brilliant light seemed to emanate from the Host, while spots of Blood appeared here and there on Its surface. Thinking that he was laboring under an illusion, he called his two acolytes and asked them what they beheld. They answered: "We see the Blood of our dear Lord on the Host." Sending for one of the Sisters who was assisting at his Mass, the priest asked her the same question, upon which she exclaimed, "A miracle!" for the strange phenomenon was visible to her eyes also. Then the other Sisters, with many lay persons, approached the altar, and all testified to the same miraculous apparition. The Blood showed Itself at five different points on the Host, representing the five different Wounds. Those who came near the altar at first saw the Blood rising to a certain height and finally congealed on the spots from which It flowed. Many people returned repeatedly to the altar to assure themselves of the reality of the vision. The priest continued the Mass and consumed the Sacred Species, but as soon as he removed the paten he noticed Blood stains on the corporal. He immediately informed the Archbishop of the singular occurrence, and the latter gave orders that the corporal should be preserved in a suitable place.

On Friday, April 29, the miracle occurred again at the seven o'clock Mass, but the priest was reticent about relating it. On Sunday, May 8, the miraculous appearance took place the third time. No word would have escaped the holy man's lips even then, had not a young seminarian who attended

Mass, being very close to the altar, told the celebrant that he had noticed some blood stains on the Host after the Consecration. This time the priest, realizing that he could no longer keep the repetition of the miracle a secret, announced it to his congregation on the Friday after Easter. Though he himself was thoroughly puzzled, he determined that if the miracle occurred again he would consecrate two Hosts, and reserve the miraculous one for future venerations.

All were awaiting a fourth manifestation of God's power and goodness. On the third Sunday after Easter the numerous worshipers, crowded in the church, noticed that after the Consecration the young seminarian repaired to the sacristy to procure another Host. Then they knew the miracle had happened and that God had shown a visible sign to His people. Sister Angelica, one of the religious attending the church, went up at once to the altar to view the miracle. She was followed by Sister Mary, and soon the entire congregation were crowding reverently about the sanctuary. The Holy Sacrifice was interrupted for twenty minutes, during which more than six hundred people witnessed the Blood oozing out of the Host and finally congealing. The pastor, repeating the words of Consecration over the new Host, finished the Mass, placed the miraculous Host on the paten and preserved It in the tabernacle.

Eight days afterwards, the author of this account, Rev. Father Julius Morel, saw the Host. He describes It as follows: "The Blood marks about the upper part of the cross on the Host had united and made one large spot. I could see the Blood oozing from the different parts, while a little of it was perceptible on the paten."

Soon afterwards, His Eminence Thomas Cardinal Gousset, Archbishop of Rheims, instituted a strict investigation into these events, and a committee having reported favorably, many pilgrimages were made to the church, where the miraculous Host was exposed for veneration.

This account is taken from three letters published in Paris in 1859 by l'Abbé Julius Morel.[1]

---

1. Brise, *Les Hosties Sanglantes de Vierge-aux-Boise.* M. l'Abbé Jules Morel, *Troise lettres* (Paris, 1859). *Sentinel of the Blessed Sacrament,* vol. XX, No. 10.

O SUBLIME Mystery, that man cannot fathom, wrought upon the altar of sacrifice! O miracle of God's power and goodness.

Prayer

HAIL, sacred tabernacles, where Thou, O Lord, dost descend at the voice of a mortal! Hail, mysterious altar, where faith comes to receive its immortal food! Oh, I love Thy temple! It is an island of peace in the ocean of the world, a beacon of immortality! Thou art near to hear us. Is there a tongue equal to the ecstasy of the heart? Whatever my lips may articulate, this blood which circulates, this bosom which breathes in Thee, this heart which beats and expands, these tear-bathed eyes, this still silence—all pray in me. So swell the waves at the rising of the King of day, so resolve the stars, mute with reverence and love, and Thou comprehendest their silent hymn. Ah, Lord, in like manner comprehend me; hear what I pronounce not. Silence is the highest voice of a heart that is overcome with Thy glory.

O happy Church! Truly in thee is a hidden God, an infinite treasure, a copious redemption, an everlasting safety. Human eye sees not, nor can any finite intelligence penetrate that ineffable, mysterious presence of Heaven's great Lord, the mighty foe to sin. *"O Salutaris Hostia, quae coeli pandis ostium!"* Wondrous things are related of Thee, to Whom nothing is impossible, Who canst in judgment or in mercy do all things in Heaven and on earth! Let weak and frail man prepare himself, then, before he enters the church. Let him think of the majesty there veiled, and presume not of himself, but seek pardon with holy fear like the publican, that with Lazarus he may deserve to find eternal rest. Let weak and frail man come here suppliantly to adore the Sacrament of Christ, not to discuss high things, or wish to penetrate difficulties, but to bow down to secret things in humble veneration, and to abandon God's mysteries to God, for Truth deceives no man—Almighty God can do all things. Amen.—*St. Paul of the Cross.*

Act of Contrition

O MY GOD I am heartily sorry for having offended Thee, because Thou art infinitely good and infinitely worthy of love, and

because sin displeases Thee. I am firmly resolved, with the help of Thy grace, never to sin again.

Spiritual Communion

MY JESUS, I believe that Thou art present in the most Blessed Sacrament. I love Thee above all things, and I desire to receive Thee into my soul. Since I cannot now receive Thee sacramentally, come at least spiritually into my heart. I embrace Thee as if Thou wert already come, and unite myself wholly to Thee. Never permit me to be separated from Thee. Amen.

Anima Christi

SOUL OF CHRIST, be my sanctification;
Body of Christ, be my salvation;
Blood of Christ, fill all my veins;
Water of Christ's side, wash out my stains;
Passion of Christ, my comfort be;
O good Jesus, listen to me;
In Thy wounds I fain would hide;
Ne'er to be parted from Thy side;
Guard me should the foe assail me;
Call me when my life shall fail me;

Bid me come to Thee above,
With Thy Saints to sing Thy love,
World without end. Amen.

Ejaculations

My God and my all!

My God, grant that I may love Thee, and be Thou the only reward of my love, to love Thee always more and more.

Holy Spirit, Spirit of Truth, come into our hearts, give to all nations the brightness of Thy light, that they may be well pleasing to Thee in the truth of faith.

A Sacred Heart Reading

Tradition relates that the soldier Longinus, who dared to plunge his lance into the Heart of Jesus, was partially blind. This misfortune, which he had endured for several years, was the result of long and severe suffering. As he withdrew his spear, a drop of divine Blood fell on his face, and at the same time his sight was restored; his soul at the same time was illumined with the light of faith, and his heart was filled with love for the God whom he had just outraged.

Longinus was not ungrateful for so great a favor: obliged to guard the Saviour's tomb after His burial, and therefore a witness to the Resurrection, he published everywhere all he had seen and heard. The Jews, being unable to corrupt him by gifts and promises, obtained an order from Pilate that he should be put to death, and two soldiers were sent to kill him. Longinus when he heard the decree leaped for joy, happy to shed his blood for Him whose Blood had cured and sanctified him. He asked for a white garment in which to celebrate the feast of his heavenly nuptials, and having embraced and blessed the two friends who escorted him to the place of execution, he was beheaded. Such was the edifying death of him who had been first the executioner, and then the apostle of the Heart of Jesus. Oh, marvelous power of the Blood which gushed from that sacred Wound! Oh, wonderful vengeance of the Redeemer! He cured miraculously both the soul and the body of the executioner. If one drop alone possessed so great a virtue, what may we not hope from that inexhaustible fountain which flows unceasingly on our altars!

MAY the Heart of Jesus in the Most Blessed Sacrament be praised, adored and loved with grateful affection, at every moment, in all the tabernacles of the world, even to the end of time! Amen.

READING 24

Story of the Blessed Sacrament (Augsburg, Bavaria—1104)

THERE exists a great number of Hosts which are recorded as miraculous because of the wonderful facts connected with them. The history of the Host of Augsburg, in Bavaria, is one of the most remarkable.

In the year 1104, an overzealous woman conceived the idea of taking a consecrated Host to her home. Accordingly, after she had received Holy Communion, she placed the Blessed Sacrament on a bit of prepared wax which she carried for the purpose in her pocket. During five years she kept the Host concealed in her apartments. At length, being forced by qualms of conscience, she openly confessed her sacrilegious deed to Father

Berthold, prior of the convent of the Holy Cross. In vain did the good priest endeavor to separate the Host from the wax. In the midst of the efforts the Host, instead of becoming loosened, took the appearance of flesh crossed by many small veins. After having sought the advice of some learned men the priest made it known to his bishop, in the meanwhile preserving the Sacred Host in a well-sealed receptacle.

Upon the recital of the event, Udalskalk, then Bishop of Augsburg, came to take the consecrated Particle in solemn procession to the Cathedral from the Church of the Holy Cross. After the wax had been removed, the onlookers were surprised to see the Host increase three times Its former size. From this time till the feast of St. John the Baptist the Sacred Host annually increased in thickness, especially during Mass, to such an extent that the wax came off by itself without any human intervention.

Bishop Udalskalk, convinced of the truth of the miracle, placed the wax, which had the appearance of human flesh, with the Blessed Sacrament in a crystal vase, and carried it in solemn procession to the Church of the Holy Cross, where it has been

preserved with the greatest reverence to the
present day. Large processions, numbering
from twenty to thirty thousand men, have
come to this church every year to adore Our
Lord in the miraculous Host.[1]

I HAVE found Him whom my soul loveth,
I hold Him and will not let Him go until
He bless me.

Prayer

O GOD, so glorious and yet so intimately
united to us, lifted so high above the heavens
and yet stooping to the lowliness of Thy creatures, so immense and yet dwelling near us
on our altars, so awful and yet so worthy
of love! Oh, for the word loud enough to
reproach the world with its blindness, coldness, and unbelief; to declare with power all
that Thou art; to cover with confusion all
those who neither believe in Thy wonderful
promise, nor in Thy wonderful gift! Thou,
O Lord, givest me too much, in giving me

---

1. Schroeder, *Bisthum Augsburg,* vol. VI. Steichele, *Arch.
de Augsburg. Cath. Encyc.,* vol. II, "Pilgrimages to Holy
Cross." Ott, *Eucharisticum.*

Thyself; for I am unworthy of so much happiness. Yet wouldst Thou give me too little in giving me anything but Thyself; for everything Thou couldst give me, with the gift of Thyself, would be too little for the satisfaction of Thy love, and all insufficient to fill my heart.

O amiable Jesus, it is in this mystery of the Blessed Sacrament that Thy charity has exerted itself in such a wonderful manner as to seem to send forth all its flames. Praise, honor and glory forever to Thy goodness and mercy! O grant, I beseech Thee, that I may duly correspond with the designs of Thy mercy, and partake of this banquet of Thy boundless love with such dispositions as are pleasing to Thee and necessary to qualify me for receiving Thy grace in so superabundant a measure as to change me entirely into Thee, that I may thus be able to say with Thine Apostle: "I live, now not I, but Christ liveth in me." Amen.—*St. John Chrysostom.*

Act of Contrition

O MY GOD I am heartily sorry for having offended Thee, because Thou art infinitely good and infinitely worthy of love, and

because sin displeases Thee. I am firmly
resolved, with the help of Thy grace, never
to sin again.

Spiritual Communion

MY JESUS, I believe that Thou art present
in the most Blessed Sacrament. I love Thee
above all things, and I desire to receive Thee
into my soul. Since I cannot now receive
Thee sacramentally, come at least spiritually
into my heart. I embrace Thee as if Thou
wert already come, and unite myself wholly
to Thee. Never permit me to be separated
from Thee. Amen.

Anima Christi

SOUL OF CHRIST, be my sanctification;
Body of Christ, be my salvation;
Blood of Christ, fill all my veins;
Water of Christ's side, wash out my stains;
Passion of Christ, my comfort be;
O good Jesus, listen to me;
In Thy wounds I fain would hide;
Ne'er to be parted from Thy side;
Guard me should the foe assail me;
Call me when my life shall fail me;

Bid me come to Thee above,
With Thy Saints to sing Thy love,
World without end. Amen.

Ejaculations

HOLY, holy, holy, Lord God of Hosts:
the earth is full of Thy glory! Glory be to
the Father, glory be to the Son, glory be to
the Holy Ghost.

Omnipotence of the Father, help my
weakness, and deliver me from the depth of
misery.

Wisdom of the Son, direct all my
thoughts, words and actions.

Love of the Holy Ghost, be Thou the
source and the beginning of all the opera-
tions of my soul, whereby they may be
always conformable to the Divine Will.

A Sacred Heart Reading

TOWARDS the end of the eleventh century
our forefathers, obedient to the voice of the
Sovereign Pontiff, formed the noble design of
checking the barbarity of the Turks, who
threatened to overrun Europe, and of deliver-
ing from their power the sepulchre of Jesus

Christ. After several splendid victories the Christians took possession of Antioch, the capital of the East, where, however, they were soon besieged by the Prince of Mossoul at the head of three hundred thousand men. Driven to desperation by hunger, the hitherto brave soldiers felt, for the first time, their courage give way. It is related in the history of the Church that a holy priest of Marseilles named Bartholomew was inspired to seek in a particular spot for the lance which had pierced the Heart of the Saviour, the finding of which would be a certain pledge of the complete triumph of the Christians over the enemy's forces. The lance was found, and preceded by this glorious token of victory the Crusaders issued forth from Antioch. At the sight of the sacred spear the Turkish troops were seized with a sudden panic; the weapons fell from their hands, they fled on all sides, and the countless dead that lay on the ground testified to their entire defeat.

From whence had the lance of Calvary drawn its strength and power? From the Heart of Jesus, which it had pierced; from the Precious Blood which it had caused to flow. But what wonders will not the Heart of Jesus effect when It deigns to dwell in our hearts in Holy Communion? By It we shall conquer all the enemies of our salvation and obtain the crown of the Blessed in Heaven.

MAY the Heart of Jesus in the Most Blessed Sacrament be praised, adored and loved with grateful affection, at every moment, in all the tabernacles of the world, even to the end of time! Amen.

READING 25

Story of the Blessed Sacrament
(Douai, France—1254)

ON the great thoroughfare leading from
Arras on to Cambrai, in the northern part
of France, lies the important town of Douai.
A priest distributing Holy Communion on
April 14, 1254, in the church of St. Ann in
this town, accidentally let one of the Particles slip from his fingers and fall to the
ground. Kneeling down with the greatest
reverence to pick It up, he saw the Sacred
Host carried to the altar by angelic hands,
and placed on the corporal. He forthwith
called the attention of the canons and the
congregation to this wonder, but when they
looked towards the altar they beheld not the
Sacred Host but a beautiful child. The news

immediately spread throughout the town, and the people hastened to the church to witness the heavenly vision.

"When I heard of it," writes Thomas Cantrimpre, to whom we are indebted for this account, "I also went to Douai, and on reaching the priest's house I asked him to take me to the church where the miracle had occurred, which he immediately did. In the meanwhile the Host had been placed in the tabernacle, but the church was still crowded with the faithful, all being most eager to get another glimpse of Our Lord. As soon as the priest opened the tabernacle, a loud cry was heard from every part of the edifice: 'He is there! See the beautiful Child, our divine Saviour!' Struck with astonishment, I stood looking into the tabernacle, for what appeared to others in the form of a child appeared to me in the usual form of bread. I wondered why I could not behold what others could see. I examined my conscience, but found that I was not guilty of any grievous sin.

"As these thoughts were passing through my mind, I too, witnessed something wonderful. Jesus Christ appeared to me as a full-grown man. On His head rested the crown of thorns, whilst Blood seemed trickling from His forehead. Instantly I fell on my knees and adored my Saviour. Then rising up, I no longer saw the crown of thorns nor the flowing Blood. His face had assumed a most majestic and venerable aspect. It was turning a little to one side so that the right eye was visible. The nose was long and straight, the eye was soft yet luminous, the hair clustering on the shoulders. The forehead was broad, but the cheeks slightly sunken. All this gave Him the appearance of an ascetic. Such was the vision I saw. For a whole hour the Sacred Host assumed various aspects, Our Lord appearing in different forms to different people. To some He seemed to be on the Cross, to others He was visibly present as a judge; but to most He appeared under the form of a little child."

Every year the citizens of Douai celebrated with great solemnity the anniversary of the day on which the vision had occurred. The feast was called "Saint-Sacrement du Miracle." Every hundred years there is a grand and impressive commemoration, extending over the space of three days. In 1792 the miraculous Host disappeared; it was believed to have been found again, but for want of certainty no honor was afterwards paid to it.[1]

O JESUS in the Most Blessed Sacrament, have mercy on us.

Prayer

My JESUS, why dost Thou love me so much? What good dost Thou see in me that Thou art so enamored of me? Hast Thou already forgotten my sins, which have offended Thee so grievously? Oh, how can I love anything else than Thee, my Jesus, my all? No one has ever done so much to make me happy, O loving, O most lovable Jesus.

O my soul, rejoice and sing a song unto the Lord! Alleluia! Praise the Lord, ye servants of God; praise ye the name of the Lord henceforth, now and forever. From the rising of the sun unto the going down of the same, the name of the Lord is worthy of praise. Who is as the Lord our God, who dwelleth on high and looketh down on the

---

1. J. Schuster, *Manual des Catechismus,* p. 323. Berzelin, *Annals of Flanders* (1615). Saraghaga, *Les Hosties de miracles. Cath. Encyc.,* vol. VII, p. 493.

low things in Heaven and on earth! Raising up the needy from the earth, and lifting up the poor out of the dunghill, that He may place them with princesses, with the princes of His people. Alleluia! Bless the Lord, O my soul, and let all that is within me bless His holy name! Bless the Lord, O my soul, and never forget all He has done for thee; who forgiveth all thy iniquities; who healeth all thy diseases; who redeemeth thy life from destruction; who crowneth thee with mercy and compassion: who satisfieth thy desires with good things. He hath not dealt with thee according to thy sins, nor rewarded thee according to thine iniquities: for, according to the height of Heaven above the earth, He has strengthened His mercy towards them that fear Him; and as far as the West is from the East, so far hath He removed our iniquities from us. Bless the Lord, all ye Angels; you that are mighty in strength and execute His word, hearkening to the voice of His orders.

Act of Contrition

O MY GOD I am heartily sorry for having offended Thee, because Thou art infinitely good and infinitely worthy of love, and because sin displeases Thee. I am firmly resolved, with the help of Thy grace, never to sin again.

Spiritual Communion

My JESUS, I believe that Thou art present in the most Blessed Sacrament. I love Thee above all things, and I desire to receive Thee into my soul. Since I cannot now receive Thee sacramentally, come at least spiritually into my heart. I embrace Thee as if Thou wert already come, and unite myself wholly to Thee. Never permit me to be separated from Thee. Amen.

Anima Christi

Soul of Christ, be my sanctification;
Body of Christ, be my salvation;
Blood of Christ, fill all my veins;
Water of Christ's side, wash out my stains;
Passion of Christ, my comfort be;
O good Jesus, listen to me;
In Thy wounds I fain would hide;
Ne'er to be parted from Thy side;
Guard me should the foe assail me;

Call me when my life shall fail me;
Bid me come to Thee above,
With Thy Saints to sing Thy love,
World without end. Amen.

Ejaculations

BENEDICTION and glory, wisdom and thanksgiving, honor, power and strength to our God forever and ever. Amen.

Jesus, Son of David, have mercy on us.
Saviour of the world, have mercy on us.

A Sacred Heart Reading

WE read a very remarkable incident in the life of St. Gertrude, whose soul was so wonderfully enlightened by Almighty God, and to whom He revealed many sublime truths. On the feast of St. John she was favored with a miraculous vision; the Beloved Disciple appeared to her at the Last Supper, leaning on the breast of the Redeemer, and at the same moment it was vouchsafed to her to experience something of the ineffable delights which flowed from the Sacred Heart of Jesus unto that of His Evangelist. St. Gertrude, addressing him, said: "Apostle of love, you had the inexpressible happiness of reposing on the bosom of Jesus, and listening to the beatings of His Heart; why, in your Gospel, did you not speak of the sentiments and adorable riches of this Divine Heart?"

"My daughter," replied St. John, "know that to me was confided the charge of instructing the infant Church concerning the person of the Incarnate Word, in order that she might transmit this fundamental truth to future ages. But God has reserved for these last times the knowledge of the delights and riches of the Heart of Jesus, so that by this means the world, when becoming old and chilled by the universal indifference of mankind, might be renovated by the fire of Divine Love."

Christians, we now live in the midst of those unhappy times of which the Beloved Disciple speaks. Alas, the fire of charity is extinguished in nearly all hearts; but let us take courage, devotion to the Sacred Heart will rekindle it!

MAY the Heart of Jesus in the Most Blessed Sacrament be praised, adored and loved with grateful affection, at every moment, in all the tabernacles of the world, even to the end of time! Amen.

READING 26

Story of the Blessed Sacrament
(Brussels, Belgium—1370)

IN THE year 1370, a wealthy Belgian
named Jonathan bribed a friend of his who
had recently become a Catholic to procure
a few consecrated Hosts. The convert
repaired to St. Catherine's church one night,
forced open the tabernacle, took the ciborium containing sixteen of the Sacred Particles, and with the stolen booty directed his
steps to Jonathan's house.

Rejoicing at his good fortune in possessing the God of the Christians, this wicked
man, with a look of scorn and derision,
threw the Sacred Hosts on the table in the
presence of his wife and son and several
other heretics. Not long after, this Jonathan

223

was killed by a band of highwaymen. His wife and son, alarmed at this dire visitation that had befallen their house, determined to take the consecrated Hosts to some of their friends in Brussels, lest perhaps a greater misfortune might befall them. These impious men surpassed Jonathan in the outrages to which they subjected the sacred species. Spreading the Sacred Hosts before them and breaking them into pieces, they were astonished to behold blood flowing copiously from several of the Particles. Struck with fear, they immediately took steps to rid themselves of the mysterious objects, and in order to accomplish their purpose, they engaged a woman, recently converted to the Catholic Faith, to inform the priest.

At that time, Wenceslaus, King of Bohemia, reigned in Brussels. When he heard of the sacrilegious robbery, the king caused those wicked men to be arrested, and according to the laws of the time, he ordered them to be executed. This happened on the eve of the Ascension of Our Lord, in the year 1370. To atone for this outrage, three of the Hosts were encased in a jeweled monstrance of gold—an offering of many princes—and borne in solemn procession to the church of St. Gudula. This procession is held annually, even up to the present time. More than thirty thousand people participated at the five-hundredth anniversary in 1870, thus making reparation during the centuries for the insults heaped upon our divine Lord in the Sacrament of His love.

The jeweled monstrance may be seen to this very day in the Zalazar chapel at St. Gudula's, upon the altar of the miraculous Sacrament. A citizen of Brussels, by the name of Giles van der Berghe, built a chapel upon the very spot where the atrocities had been committed. In this chapel three Masses are offered weekly in honor of the Most Holy Sacrament. Upon a stone over against the altar, an account of the horrid deed of the impious men is inscribed. The chapel later fell into the hands of Count Zalazar, whence the chapel derives its name. It is now the center of the Confraternity of Perpetual Adoration and of the Pious Union for supplying poor churches with altar linens and decorations for divine service.[1]

---

1. Ott, *Euch.,* p. 244. *Fastes et Legendes au S. S. per le Gaulie. Chronicles of St. Denis.* Very Rev. Couet, *Miracles Euch. Cath. Encyc.,* vol. III, p. 73b.

PRAISED and adored without end be Jesus, our love, in the Most Holy Sacrament.

Prayer

O JESUS, O most sweet Jesus, hidden under the sacramental species, give me now such love and humility that I may be able lovingly to speak of this invention of boundless love, that all who hear of it may begin to love Thee in reality.

O good Lord! O great Lord! How humbly dost Thou hide Thyself for our sake! But, alas, how much is Thy bounty and love abused! Not only do sinners despise Thee in this Sacrament of love, because they see Thee not, but the good also, the just, treat Thee with indifference and coldness. Thou hast been so long with them, and they with Thee, that for want of a lively faith they have not known Thee. Though Thou hast been with us so long, there are but few who know it, but few who are penetrated with a sense of their unspeakable happiness. I hear Thee complain of us, O dear Jesus: "Behold this Heart of Mine so full of love for men that It has shed Its last drop of

Blood for them! I have given them My own Flesh and Blood as food and drink for their souls. Consider how this Heart receives from most of men, in return for so great a love, nothing but ingratitude and contempt. But what grieves Me most is that I am thus treated even by good and just souls."

O Mary, Mother of Jesus Christ, and our dear Mother! O all ye holy angels, who, by your adoration in our churches, make up for the little love which your God and our Saviour receives from men, obtain for us the grace to comprehend a little the love of Jesus Christ in the Most Holy Sacrament.

—*St. Margaret Mary Alacoque.*

Act of Contrition

O MY GOD I am heartily sorry for having offended Thee, because Thou art infinitely good and infinitely worthy of love, and because sin displeases Thee. I am firmly resolved, with the help of Thy grace, never to sin again.

Spiritual Communion

MY JESUS, I believe that Thou art present

in the most Blessed Sacrament. I love Thee above all things, and I desire to receive Thee into my soul. Since I cannot now receive Thee sacramentally, come at least spiritually into my heart. I embrace Thee as if Thou wert already come, and unite myself wholly to Thee. Never permit me to be separated from Thee. Amen.

Anima Christi

SOUL OF CHRIST, be my sanctification;
Body of Christ, be my salvation;
Blood of Christ, fill all my veins;
Water of Christ's side, wash out my stains;
Passion of Christ, my comfort be;
O good Jesus, listen to me;
In Thy wounds I fain would hide;
Ne'er to be parted from Thy side;
Guard me should the foe assail me;
Call me when my life shall fail me;
Bid me come to Thee above,
With Thy Saints to sing Thy love,
World without end. Amen.

Ejaculations

MAY the Sacred Heart of Jesus be loved everywhere!

Jesus, my God, I love Thee above all things!

A Sacred Heart Reading

A VERY striking incident is related by the Right Reverend George Hornyold, Bishop of the diocese of York, England (1752-1778).

In the year 1760, on a day in early spring, Bishop Hornyold was on his way from Derby to Leicester with the intention of making a short episcopal visit in Higfields. Traveling on horseback all the way, he relied entirely on his gentle steed. Late in the evening he came to a crossroad; the horse at once seemed to have changed his speed and began to race down the road leading to Wittelsford in the direction of a forest. At the entrance of the woodland the horse became immovable. The rider dismounted and tethered the animal to a tree. Whilst looking for some shelter to bivouac for the night, he heard a moaning within a short distance. He tried to follow the trail of the sound and most distinctly heard: "Heart of Jesus, have mercy on me." By the light of the moon he found a man advanced in years, pale and weak, on the point of death. The Bishop braced up the dying man and gave him a swallow of wine out of his flask. On opening his eyes he cried out: "Get me a priest!" The minister of God at once made himself known, heard the poor man's confession, anointed him and gave him the Holy Viaticum: the Bishop always carried the Blessed Sacrament with him on all his trips.

After the unfortunate man had received the Sacraments, he would often whisper: "O Sacred Heart of Jesus, I thank You." Opening his eyes once more, he said: "In my youth I was very pious, but as soon as I became a soldier I went from bad to worse, and committed all kinds of sins. But in spite of my wickedness I never forgot the promise I made my mother in her dying moments to repeat daily: 'Heart of Jesus, have mercy on me,' and now the Lord has taken pity on me and sent me a priest. O Sacred Heart of Jesus, I thank You!"—and he gave up his soul to God. Bishop Hornyold now understood why his gentle horse had become so stubborn and had brought him to this place. Whilst he continued on his journey he thanked the Sacred Heart for having been so generous to a godless soldier. This incident is chronicled in the archives of the church of Leicester. The Bishop concludes in these words: "Heart of Jesus, Thou alone art good and sincere in consolation and in generosity."

MAY the Heart of Jesus in the Most Blessed Sacrament be praised, adored and loved with grateful affection, at every moment, in all the tabernacles of the world, even to the end of time! Amen.

READING 27

Story of the Blessed Sacrament
(Breslau, Germany—1831)

THE citizens of Breslau had on one occasion arranged a majestic procession of the Blessed Sacrament. Great was the devotion of the faithful as they prostrated themselves on the ground while the Blessed Sacrament proceeded along the route.

The line of march, however, passed a synagogue, where a goodly number of Hebrews had assembled. Ridicule and taunts were hurled at the Christians for adoring, as the unbelievers termed it, a small piece of bread. Not only that, but the enemies of Our Lord resolved then and there to procure a consecrated Host at any price.

Sometime later a large number of them

were congregated in a spacious dining hall, one evening, where, after having feasted and drunk freely, they determined upon securing the Sacred Particles from a church nearby. They attempted to win over the sexton of the church, but he was unwilling to become an accomplice to the wicked deed. Goaded on by his wife, however, and the lure of thirty pieces of gold, he finally consented to give a Host to the one who would accompany him to the sanctuary.

It was not long before the impious action was accomplished. The ungodly man returned to his companions and laid the consecrated Host on the table. Exultingly they told each other how they would now insult the God of the Christians. They struck the Host with their clenched fists and committed the most sacrilegious outrages. But when their diabolical frenzy was at its height, behold, to their unfeigned astonishment, the table became covered with Blood in which pieces of the Sacred Host were floating about.

So great was the clamor raised by the impious men that it attracted the attention of the police, who came to investigate and inform themselves of all that had happened.

That very night the news of the occurrence spread throughout the city, and early next morning the priest, with a large part of the congregation, entered the dining hall.

Forming a procession, amid prayers and the singing of hymns, they bore the table upon which the miracle had taken place to the church. As a result of the prodigy, some of the unbelievers embraced the Catholic Faith, whilst others, about one hundred and fifty in number, were punished according to the law of the land. Beside themselves with despair, the sexton and his wife hanged themselves. The truth of this astonishing miracle, and the result following it, are attested by John Meyer, Mayor of Breslau, and the entire history of the incident is preserved in the archives of the city hall.[1]

I ADORE Thee at every moment of my life, O Bread of Heaven, O Blessed Sacrament!

---

1. Kastner, *Geschichte des Bisthumes Breslau.* Rev. M. Mueller, C.SS.R., *Blessed Eucharist. Tabernakelwacht,* 1898.

Prayer

YES, my God, when we love Thee, something within us tells us that we are to live forever, and that the continual feast that we celebrate with Thee here on earth is but the vigil of the great eternal Feast that we are to celebrate with Thee in Heaven.

How I love those words which Thy minister pronounces as he presents me with the Eucharist Bread: May the Body of Our Lord Jesus Christ preserve thy soul unto life everlasting.—*St. Augustine.*

Act of Contrition

O MY GOD I am heartily sorry for having offended Thee, because Thou art infinitely good and infinitely worthy of love, and because sin displeases Thee. I am firmly resolved, with the help of Thy grace, never to sin again.

Spiritual Communion

MY JESUS, I believe that Thou art present in the most Blessed Sacrament. I love Thee

above all things, and I desire to receive Thee into my soul. Since I cannot now receive Thee sacramentally, come at least spiritually into my heart. I embrace Thee as if Thou wert already come, and unite myself wholly to Thee. Never permit me to be separated from Thee. Amen.

Anima Christi

SOUL OF CHRIST, be my sanctification;
Body of Christ, be my salvation;
Blood of Christ, fill all my veins;
Water of Christ's side, wash out my stains;
Passion of Christ, my comfort be;
O good Jesus, listen to me;
In Thy wounds I fain would hide;
Ne'er to be parted from Thy side;
Guard me should the foe assail me;
Call me when my life shall fail me;
Bid me come to Thee above,
With Thy Saints to sing Thy love,
World without end. Amen.

Ejaculations

MAY the Sacred Heart of Jesus be loved everywhere.

Most merciful Jesus, Lover of souls! I pray Thee, by the agony of Thy Most Sacred Heart, and by the sorrows of Thine Immaculate Mother, wash in Thy Blood the sinners of the whole world who are now in their agony, and are to die this day. Amen.

Heart of Jesus, once in agony, have mercy on the dying.

A Sacred Heart Reading

THE following incident, which took place in Canada in the year 1872, proves how good and merciful is the Heart of Jesus.

A man, advanced in years, had given up frequenting the Sacraments for more than thirty years, and not only was he indifferent as to his religious duties, but he was also animated by a dislike and hatred of priests; on every occasion he sought to speak against them, and to turn into ridicule both themselves and their holy office. For many years his family prayed earnestly for his conversion, but in vain. At length a relative known for her piety was inspired with the idea of appealing, as a last resource, to the Sacred Heart of Jesus, to which she had a great devotion. She hastened to the church, obtained a blessed medal of the Sacred Heart, and on her return hid it in the clothes of the poor sinner. Her next thought was to have several novenas made in different convents; and after a time, trusting that the united supplications had prevailed with the merciful Heart of her good Master, she sent for a priest, and contrived a meeting between him and the lost sheep she hoped to restore to the fold.

The triumph of grace was complete and miraculous. The sinner, who for so many years had hated the sight of a priest, eagerly welcomed this one; he made his confession with contrition and faith, and from that time he was most zealous in prayer and works of piety. The family was overjoyed, and the new convert was most grateful to the Heart of Jesus, which had withdrawn him from the brink of Hell.

MAY the Heart of Jesus in the Most Blessed Sacrament be praised, adored and loved with grateful affection, at every moment, in all the tabernacles of the world, even to the end of time! Amen.

READING 28

Story of the Blessed Sacrament
(Guadalupe, Spain—1640)

A WORK called the *Divine Wonders of the Blessed Sacrament,* published in Paris in 1859, brings to notice an authentic document drawn up by the Venerable Peter, Prior of Guadalupe, Spain, in which he confirmed a miracle that happened to him while celebrating Mass.

This holy monk, who was a member of the Order of St. Jerome, was at one time strongly tempted to doubt the Real Presence of Jesus under the sacramental species. Day after day he was tormented by thoughts of distrust, yet he committed no sin, for deep in his heart he believed in the holy doctrine.

It happened on Saturday that he was

celebrating Holy Mass in honor of our Blessed Lady. Bowing down before the altar in the customary manner after the Consecration, he reverently recited the prayer, "We suppliantly beseech Thee." What was his astonishment when he raised his eyes to behold a wonderful cloud enveloping the altar and hiding the sacred species from his gaze!

The good Father was beside himself with amazement. He felt his blood congeal in his veins, and was so much disturbed that he hesitated before continuing the Mass. With a fervent prayer he besought Our Lord's forgiveness for his incredulity. Hardly had he concluded his supplication when the cloud seemed to rise and vanish from his sight.

On close inspection he found that the Sacred Host was no longer lying on the corporal, nor was there a drop of Blood in the uncovered chalice. Again having recourse to the all-merciful God, he asked pardon for his unbelief and acknowledged his utter unworthiness to offer up the Holy Sacrifice. In his distress, with suppliant attitude, he turned to the Mother of God, in whose honor he was celebrating the Mass. Then

raising his eyes, he noticed in the air the
brilliant paten, from which proceeded rays
of light illuminating the church. Slowly the
golden disk descended, bearing on its surface the Sacred Host. As it rested in an
upright position over the chalice, he dis-
cerned drops of Blood trickling from the
sacramental Particle and falling into the
chalice, until the quantity therein was equal
to that of the wine he had used at the Offer-
tory. Then the Host descended upon the
corporal, while the pall, without the aid of
human hands, covered the chalice.

At the sight of these wonders, the good
priest, being very much puzzled, knew not
what to do. But immediately a low voice
whispered to him, saying, "Continue the
Mass, and keep as a profound secret that
which you have seen, for it was for you
alone that God granted this vision, that you
might no longer doubt the Real Presence of
the Lord Jesus Christ under each of the
appearances of bread and wine."

Until the day of his death the holy man
kept this heavenly secret, but as he was
about to leave the world he considered that,
for the glory of God and the confirmation
of faith in the Real Presence, it might be well

to leave this simple record to others who might be tempted to doubt as he did.[1]

O SACRAMENT most holy, O Sacrament divine! All praise and all thanksgiving be every moment Thine.

Prayer

IT is obedience, O my God, which brings me to Thy holy table: even the tender words by which Thou invitest us could not have induced me to come; for, in the trouble of my soul, I could not judge if they were addressed to me. Misery and infirmities entitle one to admission to Thy banquet, but nothing can dispense us from the nuptial robe; and when I cast my eyes on myself, after having raised them to Thee, I doubt, I hesitate, and I tremble; because if I absent myself, I fly from life; if I approach unworthily, I add sacrilege to my sins. But Thy merciful wisdom, O my God, in forseeing all our weakness: it has prepared help

---

1. *Historia de la Aparicion: Anticoli.* Jos. Soli, *Les Merveilles Divines,* lii.

against both presumption and despair. I
obey, then, O my God; and in the midst of
the darkness which surrounds me, I will
blindly follow the guide Thou hast given me
to Thee; I will approach Thine altar without
desiring any other testimony of my innocence than these words which come from
his lips, or rather from Thine: *You may go
to Holy Communion.—St. Augustine.*

Act of Contrition

O MY GOD I am heartily sorry for having
offended Thee, because Thou art infinitely
good and infinitely worthy of love, and
because sin displeases Thee. I am firmly
resolved, with the help of Thy grace, never
to sin again.

Spiritual Communion

MY JESUS, I believe that Thou art present
in the most Blessed Sacrament. I love Thee
above all things, and I desire to receive Thee
into my soul. Since I cannot now receive
Thee sacramentally, come at least spiritually
into my heart. I embrace Thee as if Thou
wert already come, and unite myself wholly

to Thee. Never permit me to be separated
from Thee. Amen.

Anima Christi

SOUL OF CHRIST, be my sanctification;
Body of Christ, be my salvation;
Blood of Christ, fill all my veins;
Water of Christ's side, wash out my stains;
Passion of Christ, my comfort be;
O good Jesus, listen to me;
In Thy wounds I fain would hide;
Ne'er to be parted from Thy side;
Guard me should the foe assail me;
Call me when my life shall fail me;
Bid me come to Thee above,
With Thy Saints to sing Thy love,
World without end. Amen.

Ejaculations

I ADORE Thee at every moment of my life,
O Bread of Heaven, O Blessed Sacrament!

Divine Jesus, heart of Mary, bless me, I
beseech Thee.

I give Thee, O sweetest Saviour, my soul
forever. May the Most Holy and Most
Divine Sacrament be known, adored and

thanked at every moment by all.

A Sacred Heart Reading

FIDELITY to the Catholic Faith was considered high treason in England during the religious persecution of the fifteenth and sixteenth centuries. The faithful were branded with the name of traitor, and as such they were treated at the public tribunal of justice, as well as under the tortures of their executioners. The ordinary punishment was that of hanging on the common gallows; the cord was then severed, and the victims fell to the ground, still breathing. Then the hangman, armed with a sharp knife, approached the culprit, and plunging the blade into his heart, pulled out the quivering heart, and showing it to the assembled crowd, cried out: "Behold the heart of a traitor!" It is related that a priest, about to expire under this atrocious mode of torture, collected all his remaining strength, and whilst the executioner searched for his throbbing heart, gave the following magnificent denial to his words: "Know that which thou holdest in thy hand is not the heart of a traitor, but a heart consecrated to

God." His last breath was an act of divine love.

Would to Heaven, O Christian, that when on the day of your death you feel in your breast the last feeble pulsations of your heart, you may be able to resist the demon's hand and to cry: "Begone, Satan, begone! This heart does not belong to you. Neither the world nor the passions have sullied it. My heart has throbbed only for the Heart of Jesus."

MAY the Heart of Jesus in the Most Blessed Sacrament be praised, adored and loved with grateful affection, at every moment, in all the tabernacles of the world, even to the end of time! Amen.

READING 29

Story of the Blessed Sacrament
(Posen, Poland—1599)

IN the Church of San Lorenzo, Milan, Italy, there is a famous painting by the renowned artist Delloti, a copy of which may be seen in the Eucharistic Museum, Paray-le-Monial. It represents a historic fact.

About the year 1599, in the city of Posen, a very remarkable incident took place in connection with the Blessed Sacrament. A servant girl, who was bribed by some unbelievers, stole from the chapel of the Dominicans three small Hosts, wrapped them in a linen cloth, and carried them to the house of the wretches who had hired her for the deed. The unbelievers treated the Sacred Hosts in a most sacrilegious and shameful manner. They threw them on a table and cut the Sacred Particles. Blood spurted out on the first one of the sacrilegious creatures and left a stain that could not be removed. The report of this strange occurrence soon spread abroad and crowds ran to see for themselves. A blind woman insisted on being led to the scene of this marvelous incident. Divinely inspired, she cried out: "If Thou art the true God, He whom our ancestors nailed to the Cross, restore to me my sight!" She was immediately cured, and went away proclaiming the miracle. The guilty profaners, fearing the just punishment of their heinous crime, wished to dispose of the desecrated Hosts, and after several fruitless efforts buried them to a great depth in a swamp.

One day on the octave of the Blessed Virgin, two herdsmen, father and son, brought their cattle to pasture near this place. The father went to a church not far off to hear Mass, while the son guarded the herd. To his surprise the boy saw the cattle approach the swamp and kneel down with their heads bent low. The shepherd raised his eyes and saw in the air over the swamp three shining objects. In amazement he perceived that they

were three Hosts, and he instantly prostrated himself and profoundly adored the
God who revealed Himself by so great a
prodigy.

In the meantime, the father returned from
Mass. As soon as the boy saw him he ran
to meet him. "Father," he shouted, "our
oxen are adoring the Blessed Sacrament!"
"Nonsense!" replied the parent, shrugging
his shoulders, "what folly is this!" "Come
and see for yourself," protested the boy,
"that I am telling the truth." While proceeding on his way the old man suddenly
paused, with feet fastened to the ground and
with eyes entranced as he beheld the
astonishing scene. There at the farthest end
of the marsh three little lights hung in the
air, while the dumb beasts knelt with heads
bowed to the earth. The old herdsman, all
doubts gone, knelt in adoration before the
three consecrated Hosts profaned by the
unbelievers.

After a moment's prayer, the old man ran
to the city and proclaimed the wonder to all
whom he met. The people, however, looked
upon *him* as a fool, and even cast him into
prison. And now a new wonder occurred—
the prison door opened and freed the pris-

oner. This startled the authorities and they began to investigate. The Bishop and the clergy were informed and went in procession to the place indicated by the herdsman. Then the Sacred Hosts, which had remained suspended in the air, slowly descended and rested in the hands of a saintly priest. They were taken back to the city amidst great pomp and splendor. Then the authorities began to debate what disposition to make of the miraculous Hosts. While they were arguing, the Hosts rose from their hands, ascended into the air and returned to the marsh. The wish of Our Lord was evident. So they erected an improvised sanctuary on the spot, and this in turn was soon followed by a magnificent basilica founded by Ladislaus Jagellon, King of Poland. Needless to say, thousands of pilgrims have visited the famous shrine to adore the miraculous Hosts.[1]

PRAISED and blessed forever be the most holy and divine Sacrament!

---

1. Rosmini, *Historia de Milano,* p. 135. *Zeitschrift der Historischen Gesellschaft* (Munich, 1850). *Les Merveilles de S. Eucharistie* (Paris, 1875).

Prayer

O MY SAVIOUR, what clearness, what precision, what force, but at the same time, what authority and what power in Thy words! "Woman, thou art healed," and that same instant she is healed. *"This is My Body!"* It is His Body. *"This is My Blood!"* It is His Blood.

Who could speak in this manner but He who holds everything in His hand? Who could make Himself believed, if not He to whom to speak and to act are the same thing? My soul, pause here in silence; believe simply, as strongly as thy Saviour has spoken, with as much submission as He displays authority and power.

Who could possibly explain the prodigies that Thine omnipotence works in this Sacrament? Those which were performed by Thee, O my Saviour, almost during Thine entire life, had their own time and their own particular place; but Thou renewest the miracles of the Holy Eucharist every day, every hour, and in an infinity of places. There Thou art enclosed in a little Host. Thou art at one and the same time in

Heaven, seated at the right hand of the Father, and in millions of places, always the same and always entire. These are the daily miracles of Thy love for us. It is here, Lord, that I am forced to cry out with St. Thomas: "My Lord and my God!" Amen.—*Bossuet.*

Act of Contrition

O MY GOD I am heartily sorry for having offended Thee, because Thou art infinitely good and infinitely worthy of love, and because sin displeases Thee. I am firmly resolved, with the help of Thy grace, never to sin again.

Spiritual Communion

MY JESUS, I believe that Thou art present in the most Blessed Sacrament. I love Thee above all things, and I desire to receive Thee into my soul. Since I cannot now receive Thee sacramentally, come at least spiritually into my heart. I embrace Thee as if Thou wert already come, and unite myself wholly to Thee. Never permit me to be separated from Thee. Amen.

Anima Christi

SOUL OF CHRIST, be my sanctification;
Body of Christ, be my salvation;
Blood of Christ, fill all my veins;
Water of Christ's side, wash out my stains;
Passion of Christ, my comfort be;
O good Jesus, listen to me;
In Thy wounds I fain would hide;
Ne'er to be parted from Thy side;
Guard me should the foe assail me;
Call me when my life shall fail me;
Bid me come to Thee above,
With Thy Saints to sing Thy love,
World without end. Amen.

Ejaculation

MAKE me a clean heart, O God, and
renew a right spirit within me. Cast me not
away from Thy presence and take not Thy
Holy Spirit from me. Oh, give me the comfort of Thy help again, and establish me
with Thy free Spirit. Amen.

A Sacred Heart Reading

DURING the month of May, 1722, the plague broke out in the town of Marseilles. Death, the king of terrors, erected his mournful throne in the midst of that great city, once so brilliant and so gay. Deserted by all the inhabitants who had it in their power to fly, Marseilles soon became like a battlefield, strewn with the dying and the dead. The afflicted town saw her streets and public places blocked by its victims, priests and doctors decimated by the dreadful visitation, and forty thousand persons consigned to the grave. It was then that the holy Bishop of Marseilles, Monsignor Belzunce —a model of charity and pastoral zeal—was inspired with the idea of having recourse to the Sacred Heart of Jesus, of consecrating to It the unfortunate town and diocese, and of establishing in Its honor a solemn and public procession in perpetuity. The magistrates and the people joined in the vow of the venerable prelate, which already gave promise to a speedy deliverance. Marseilles was consecrated to the Sacred Heart, and the procession took place with every demonstration of religious pomp. Suddenly the plague ceased; fear vanished and the inhabitants returned, and during six weeks not a single death, or sickness of any sort, was known in the town. "Oh, you whose lives are spent on the waters of the ocean," said the Bishop, addressing the sailors of Marseilles, "publish to all nations, even the most uncivilized, the glory, power and infinite mercy of the Sacred Heart of Jesus, which has worked such wonders in our behalf and has turned our sorrows into joys."

MAY the Heart of Jesus in the Most Blessed Sacrament be praised, adored and loved with grateful affection, at every moment, in all the tabernacles of the world, even to the end of time! Amen.

READING 30

Story of the Blessed Sacrament (Louvain, Belgium—1374)

THIS account is taken from *The Messenger of the Sacred Heart,* September, 1908, signed by Ferdinand C. Wheeler, S. J.

The remembrance of an act of God's condescension exists in the parochial church of St. Jacques, Louvain. In a special repository to the left of the high altar is preserved the Sacrament of the Miracle, a consecrated Host that more than five hundred years ago was changed into visible flesh. In that Host Our Lord has received the pious homage of the faithful and He in turn has given them His choicest gifts, until today the insult once offered to the Hidden Presence has about been forgotten.

The miracle took place in Middleburg, the capital of Zealand. A noble lady of that city was accustomed in a special way to look after the spiritual welfare of her domestics, and by her counsel and exhortations induced them to approach the Sacraments at regular intervals. One of them, named John, a native of Cologne, by his disorderly life caused great pain to his mistress. In the year 1374 the pious lady, according to custom, wished all her servants to receive the Sacraments on the First Sunday of Lent. From fear of falling into disfavor, John, too, went to the church on the appointed day, and without first going to Confession approached the Holy Table. Hardly had the priest placed the Sacred Host upon his unholy tongue than It was miraculously transformed into a morsel of visible Flesh. The sacrilegious man, unable to swallow It and wishing to hide his crime, dared to bite the miraculous Flesh. Three drops of Blood fell from his lips upon the Communion cloth. Immediately the priest, filled with horror at the spectacle, snatched the sacred species from the profaner's mouth and reverently replaced It in the ciborium which he held in his hand.

Nor was God's anger slow to descend

upon the unhappy sinner. In an instant he was stricken blind. Then the enormity of his present sin, coupled with all the irregularities of his past life, broke in upon his soul. With a cry to God for mercy he fell at the priest's feet and confessed his sins before all the people. God saw his repentance and restored his sight. John rose up a new man and ever after remained faithful to his resolution of leading a life of devotion to the Blessed Sacrament.

During five hundred years and more the Blessed Sacrament of the Miracle has been honored at Louvain with jubilees and processions and annual feasts of every kind.

The Augustinians at Louvain were several times driven from their convent during the French Revolution. Their first care was to bring the precious relic into some safe place. In 1803 the Miraculous Host was placed in the church of the hospital served by the nuns of St. Augustine, whence It was afterwards transferred to the church of St. Jacques, where It now rests. Around the walls of the church are paintings which give the different scenes in the history of the miracle.

Today this Host, changed into visible

Flesh, has a brownish color. It has shrunk into the shape of a small ball, about the size of an ordinary pea, but one can easily perceive that It is of flesh. When the precious Treasure is carried in procession or exposed upon the altar, a consecrated Host is placed in the monstrance behind It.

O SACRAMENT most holy! O Sacrament divine! All praise and all thanksgiving be every moment Thine.

Prayer

O JESUS, my God and my Saviour, with that lowly homage with which faith inspires me, I worship Thee, true God and true Man; with my whole heart I love Thee, enclosed in the most august Sacrament of the Altar, in reparation for all the acts of irreverence, profanation and sacrilege which, to my shame, I may ever have committed, as well as for those which have ever been committed, or ever may be committed in ages to come.

I adore Thee, my God, not indeed as much as Thou deservest or as much as I ought, but according to the little strength I have; and fain would I adore Thee with all the perfection of every rational creature. Meanwhile, I purpose, now and forever, to adore Thee, not only for those Catholics who adore Thee not and love Thee not, but also for the conversion of all heretics, schismatics, Mohammedans, Jews, idolaters and wicked Christians. Ah, my Jesus, may all men ever know, adore, love and praise Thee every moment in the most holy and most Divine Sacrament! Amen.

Act of Contrition

O MY GOD I am heartily sorry for having offended Thee, because Thou art infinitely good and infinitely worthy of love, and because sin displeases Thee. I am firmly resolved, with the help of Thy grace, never to sin again.

Spiritual Communion

MY JESUS, I believe that Thou art present in the most Blessed Sacrament. I love Thee above all things, and I desire to receive Thee into my soul. Since I cannot now receive Thee sacramentally, come at least spiritually into my heart. I embrace Thee as if Thou wert already come, and unite myself wholly to Thee. Never permit me to be separated from Thee. Amen.

Anima Christi

SOUL OF CHRIST, be my sanctification;
Body of Christ, be my salvation;
Blood of Christ, fill all my veins;
Water of Christ's side, wash out my stains;
Passion of Christ, my comfort be;
O good Jesus, listen to me;
In Thy wounds I fain would hide;
Ne'er to be parted from Thy side;
Guard me should the foe assail me;
Call me when my life shall fail me;
Bid me come to Thee above,
With Thy Saints to sing Thy love,
World without end. Amen.

Ejaculations

I ADORE THEE at every moment, O living Bread of Heaven, O great Sacrament.

Jesus, heart of Mary, I pray Thee, bless my soul.

A Sacred Heart Reading

A PERSON known for his devotion to the Heart of Jesus related the following circumstances. "My grandfather, when eighty years of age, fell dangerously ill. Unfortunately he was an atheist, who believed neither in the existence of God nor the immortality of the soul; he had never had the happiness of making his first Holy Communion. I endeavored to speak to him of the necessity and beauty of the Catholic religion, and particularly of the future state of the soul, but all my arguments were useless. The month of June was about to begin; I resolved to sanctify it, and to invoke daily the Sacred Heart of Jesus for the conversion of this poor sinner. My supplications were not in vain; on the first day of this blessed month, the merciful Heart of Jesus granted my request, for that evening the parish priest was seen by the bedside of the sick man, instructing him in the principal mysteries of religion. The next day, my grandfather made his confession and received absolution, after which he affectionately thanked the priest, saying: 'Oh, how happy you have made me!' The day fixed for his first Holy Communion was the fourth of June; he was then to receive that God so long unknown to him. Children, grandchildren surrounded his bed. He afterwards sat up, embraced us all, and wept with joy and happiness. This was not the only favor granted by the Heart of Jesus; for grace was given him to expiate, by much suffering, a life of sin, and this soul passed from life on the last day of the month dedicated to the most Sacred Heart of Jesus."

How true it is that we can obtain all we desire during this month of graces, if we invoke the Heart of Jesus with fervor and perseverance.

M AY the Heart of Jesus in the Most Blessed Sacrament be praised, adored and loved with grateful affection, at every moment, in all the tabernacles of the world, even to the end of time! Amen.

LITANIES AND OTHER PRAYERS

Litany of the Holy Name of Jesus
(For public or private use.)

LORD, have mercy on us.
Christ, have mercy on us.
Lord, have mercy on us. Jesus, hear us.
Jesus, graciously hear us.
God the Father of Heaven,
Have mercy on us.
God the Son, Redeemer of the world,
Have mercy on us.
God the Holy Ghost,
Have mercy on us.
Holy Trinity, One God,
Have mercy on us.

Jesus, Son of the living God,
Have mercy on us.

Jesus, splendor of the Father,
   Have mercy on us.
Jesus, brightness of eternal light, *etc.*
Jesus, King of glory,
Jesus, Sun of justice,
Jesus, Son of the Virgin Mary,
Jesus, most amiable,
Jesus, most admirable,
Jesus, mighty God,
Jesus, Father of the world to come,
Jesus, Angel of great counsel,
Jesus, most powerful,
Jesus, most patient,
Jesus, most obedient,
Jesus, meek and humble of heart,
Jesus, Lover of chastity,
Jesus, Lover of us,
Jesus, God of peace,
Jesus, Author of life,
Jesus, Model of virtues,
Jesus, zealous for souls,
Jesus, our God,
Jesus, our Refuge,
Jesus, Father of the poor,
Jesus, Treasure of the faithful,
Jesus, Good Shepherd,
Jesus, true Light,
Jesus, eternal Wisdom,

Jesus, infinite Goodness,
Jesus, our Way and our Life,
Jesus, Joy of Angels,
Jesus, King of Patriarchs,
Jesus, Master of Apostles,
Jesus, Teacher of Evangelists,
Jesus, Strength of Martyrs,
Jesus, Light of Confessors,
Jesus, Purity of Virgins,
Jesus, Crown of all Saints,

Be merciful,
  Spare us, O Jesus.
Be merciful,
  Graciously hear us, O Jesus.

From all evil,
  Jesus, deliver us.
From all sin,
  Jesus, deliver us.
From Thy wrath, *etc.*
From the snares of the devil,
From the spirit of fornication,
From everlasting death,
From the neglect of Thine inspirations,
Through the mystery of Thy holy
  Incarnation,
Through Thy Nativity,

Through Thine Infancy,
Through Thy most divine life,
Through Thy labors,
Through Thine Agony and Passion,
Through Thy Cross and dereliction,
Through Thy faintness and weariness,
Through Thy death and burial,
Through Thy Resurrection,
Through Thine Ascension,
Through Thine institution of the Most Holy
　　Eucharist,
Through Thy joys,
Through Thy glory,

Lamb of God, Who takest away the sins of
　　the world,
　　Spare us, O Jesus.
Lamb of God, Who takest away the sins of
　　the world,
　　Hear us, O Jesus.
Lamb of God, Who takest away the sins of
　　the world,
　　Have mercy on us, O Jesus.

V. Jesus, hear us,
R. *Jesus, graciously hear us.*

Let us Pray

O Lord Jesus Christ, Who hast said: "Ask and ye shall receive; seek, and ye shall find; knock, and it shall be opened unto you"; grant, we beseech Thee, to us who ask, the gift of Thy most divine love, that we may ever love Thee with all our heart, and in all our words and actions, and never cease from praising Thee.

Make us, O Lord, to have both a perpetual fear and love of Thy holy name, for Thou never failest to govern those whom Thou foundest upon the strength of Thy love, Who livest and reignest, world without end. R. *Amen.*

Litany of the Sacred Heart of Jesus
(For public or private use.)

LORD, have mercy on us.
  Christ, have mercy on us.
Lord, have mercy on us. Christ, hear us.
  Christ, graciously hear us.
God the Father of Heaven,
  Have mercy on us.
God the Son, Redeemer of the world,
  Have mercy on us.

God the Holy Ghost,
Have mercy on us.
Holy Trinity, One God,
Have mercy on us.

Heart of Jesus, Son of the eternal Father,
Have mercy on us.
Heart of Jesus, formed by the Holy Ghost
in the womb of the Virgin Mother,
Have mercy on us.
Heart of Jesus, substantially united to the
Word of God, *etc.*
Heart of Jesus, of infinite majesty,
Heart of Jesus, holy Temple of God,
Heart of Jesus, Tabernacle of the Most
High,
Heart of Jesus, House of God and Gate of
Heaven,
Heart of Jesus, burning Furnace of charity,
Heart of Jesus, Abyss of all virtues,
Heart of Jesus, most worthy of all praise,
Heart of Jesus, King and center of all hearts,
Heart of Jesus, in Whom are all the treas-
ures of wisdom and knowledge,
Heart of Jesus, in Whom dwelleth all the
fullness of the divinity,
Heart of Jesus, in Whom the Father was
well pleased,

Heart of Jesus, of whose fullness we have all received,

Heart of Jesus, desire of the everlasting hills,

Heart of Jesus, patient and abounding in mercy,

Heart of Jesus, rich unto all who call upon Thee,

Heart of Jesus, Fountain of life and holiness,

Heart of Jesus, Propitiation for our sins,

Heart of Jesus, filled with reproaches,

Heart of Jesus, bruised for our offenses,

Heart of Jesus, made obedient unto death,

Heart of Jesus, pierced with a lance,

Heart of Jesus, Source of all consolation,

Heart of Jesus, our Life and Resurrection,

Heart of Jesus, our Peace and Reconciliation,

Heart of Jesus, Victim for our sins,

Heart of Jesus, Salvation of those who hope in Thee,

Heart of Jesus, Hope of those who die in Thee,

Heart of Jesus, Delight of all the saints,

Lamb of God, Who takest away the sins of the world,
Spare us, O Lord.

Lamb of God, Who takest away the sins of
the world,
Graciously hear us, O Lord.
Lamb of God, Who takest away the sins of
the world,
Have mercy on us.

V. Jesus, meek and humble of heart,
R. *Make our hearts like unto Thine.*

Let us Pray

O Almighty and eternal God, consider
the Heart of Thy well-beloved Son and the
praises and satisfaction He offers Thee in the
name of sinners; appeased by worthy homage, pardon those who implore Thy mercy,
in the name of the same Jesus Christ Thy
Son, Who lives and reigns with Thee, world
without end. R. *Amen.*

Prayer for Divine Love

O GOD, Who dost possess in incomprehensible abundance all that can ever be perfect and worthy of love, extinguish in me all
culpable, sensual and disorderly love for
creatures, and enkindle in my heart the most
pure fire of Thy sincere, powerful and con-

tinual love, in order that I may love nothing save Thee alone, or for Thee, until, consumed by Thy most holy love, I may begin to live where I shall perfectly possess Thee, with all Thy elect, and love Thee without end. Amen. —*St. Bonaventure.*

Prayer Before the Altar

O DIVINE SAVIOUR, Who dost admit me to Thy presence! Teach me to respect as I ought the sanctity of Thy house, to feel delight in it as Thy Saints did and to pray to Thee with the same fervor, so that I may be able to say, like them: "We have received Thy mercy, O Lord, in the midst of Thy temple. Oh, grant that, rendering Thee the worship of love that they rendered Thee, I too may deserve to experience Thy mercy in that eternal temple of which our churches are the figure, and where Thy presence brings sovereign happiness." Amen. —*Fenelon.*

Mystical Prayer of Blessed Angela

O ADMIRABLE ONE, Thou dost work marvels in Thy children. O Supernal Good! O incomprehensible and most burning

Charity! O Thou Divine Person Who hast deigned to *substantify* us in the midst of Thy substance! O wonder of all wonders that Thou workest in Thy children! O hidden marvel, incomprehensible to us poor mortal beings! By Thy grace and the light of God we feel this substance; and to all true solitaries it is a pledge of their betrothal, and all the choirs of the angels are occupied therein, and all they too who are true contemplatives shall occupy themselves therein, and afterwards they shall be solitaries, and separated from the earth, whose conversation is in Heaven. Thanks be to God.

—*Blessed Angela of Foligno.*

Prayer Before the Tabernacle

ETERNAL SON of the living God, Whom I here acknowledge really present! I adore Thee with all the powers of my soul.

Prostrate with the Angels in the most profound reverence, I love Thee, O my Saviour, Whom I now behold on the throne of Thy love!

O dread Majesty, O infinite Mercy! Save me, forgive me! Grant that I may never more be separated from Thee. —*St. Basil.*

Prayer of Adoration
Of the Most Blessed Sacrament

O SOVEREIGN LORD! What do I now behold? All Thy greatness concealed under the veil of bread! And while Thy love for us ungrateful sinners reduces Thee so low, the heavens are astonished, the Angels tremble, the Seraphim cover their faces. All the powers of the universe bow down in adoration and praise, and with a thousand voices exalt Thine infinite Majesty, which fills both Heaven and earth.

Christian people, let us unite our voices with theirs and publish to the whole world this sublime and eternal canticle: Holy, holy, holy is the powerful God of armies! The heavens and the earth are filled with His glory. Let us bless Him that cometh in the name of the Lord, who is the Lord Himself. Amen. *—St. Hilary.*

Petition for Perfect Divine Love

M Y GOD, Thou art here present. Show Thyself to me. Reveal to me Thy beauty. Let me have the happiness of embracing Thee,

and of being intimately united with Thee.
Grant that I may make one of those acts of
love that are capable of perfectly cleansing
the greatest sinners from all the stains of sin
and of rendering them worthy of being
admitted without delay into Heaven. Grant
that I may be continually united with Thee.
Amen.   —*St. Bonaventure.*

Litany for a Happy Death

O LORD JESUS, God of goodness and
Father of mercies! I approach Thee with a
contrite and humble heart. To Thee do I
recommend the last hour of my life and the
decision of my eternal destiny.

When my feet benumbed with death shall
admonish me that my mortal course is
drawing to an end,

Merciful Jesus, have mercy on me.

When my trembling hands shall no longer
be able to press the crucifix to my heart and,
despite my efforts, shall let it fall on my bed
of sorrow,

Merciful Jesus, have mercy on me.

When my eyes, dim and troubled at the
approach of death, shall fix themselves on
Thee, my last and only support,

Merciful Jesus, have mercy on me.

When my ears, soon to be forever shut to the discourse of man, shall be opened to hear the irrevocable decree which is to cut me off from the number of the living,

Merciful Jesus, have mercy on me.

When my lips, cold and trembling, shall pronounce for the last time Thine adorable name,

Merciful Jesus, have mercy on me.

When my heart, yielding to the pressure and exhausted by its frequent struggles against the enemies of its salvation, shall feel the pangs of death,

Merciful Jesus, have mercy on me.

When my friends and relations, encircling my bed, shall shed a tear over me and invoke Thy clemency in my behalf,

Merciful Jesus, have mercy on me.

When I shall have lost the use of my senses; when the world shall have vanished from my sight; when my agonizing soul feels the sorrows of death,

Merciful Jesus, have mercy on me.

When my soul, trembling on my lips, shall bid adieu to the world and leave my body lifeless, pale and cold, receive this separation as an homage which I willingly pay to Thy Divine Majesty; and in that last moment of my mortal life,

Merciful Jesus, have mercy on me.

When at length my soul, admitted to Thy presence, shall first behold the splendor of Thy Majesty, reject me not, but receive me into Thy bosom, where I may forever sing Thy praises; and in that moment when eternity shall begin for me,

Merciful Jesus, have mercy on me. Amen.

Prayer for a Happy Death

SWEET LORD, when our turn comes to die, grant that we may sleep calmly the sleep of the just. Guard us from the enemy; save us from the pit. Let our friends remember us and pray for us, so that the pains of Purgatory, so much deserved by us, and therefore so truly welcomed by us, may be over with little delay. Give us season of refreshments there; wrap us around with holy dreams and soothing contemplations, while we gather strength to ascend the heavens.

—*Cardinal Newman.*

Prayer for the Dying

O MOST merciful Jesus, Lover of souls, I pray Thee, by the agony of Thy most Sacred Heart and by the sorrows of Thine Immaculate Mother, wash in Thy Blood the sinners of the whole world who are in their agony and are to die this day. Amen.

—*St. Francis de Sales.*

HEART OF JESUS once in agony, have pity on the dying.

Eternal Father, I offer Thee the Precious Blood of Jesus in satisfaction for my sins and for the needs of Holy Church.

—*St. Cyprian.*

Act of Faith in the Real Presence

O MY JESUS, dwelling in the Blessed Sacrament, as the meanest of Thy creatures, lost in my own nothingness, prostrate before the throne of Thy great Majesty, profoundly do I adore Thee with all my spirit, with all the powers of my soul; and here I acknowledge Thee, veiled beneath the sacramental species, as my God, my Creator, my last end. With true and living faith I believe that in this adorable Sacrament Thou Thyself, true God and true Man, art present, Who being the sole-begotten Son of God didst yet, from Thy great love for man, take to Thyself human flesh in the most pure womb of Mary ever virgin, by the operation of the Holy Ghost; therefore wast Thou born poor, in a vile manger; therefore didst Thou live subject to men. And now that, having conquered death and Hell, Thou dost sit glorious at the right hand of Thy Father, I believe that, without abandoning the heavenly throne of Thy glory, Thou dost yet dwell substantially and really in this ineffable Sacrament, wherein I glorify Thee as God in the firmament of Thy Church, as the Lamb enthroned upon His seat of love, as the Priest of the sanctuary of all grace, as the sweet Manna of all consolation and as the Arbiter of my eternal fate in this court of mercy. Yes, my dear Jesus, all this I declare and believe, as Thou hast commanded me, and as Thy spouse, the Catholic Church, my mother, teaches. Amen.

—*St. Philip Neri.*

BENEDICTION OF THE MOST BLESSED SACRAMENT

O Salutaris Hostia

O Salutaris Hostia,
  Quae coeli pandis ostium:
Bella premunt hostilia
  Da robur, fer auxilium.

Uni trinoque Domino
  Sit sempiterna gloria:
Qui vitam sine termino,
  Nobis donet in patria. Amen.

O Saving Victim
(English version of the O Salutaris Hostia.)

O Saving Victim, opening wide
  The gate of Heaven to man below;
Our foes press on from every side;

Thine aid supply, Thy strength bestow.

To Thy great Name be endless praise,
  Immortal Godhead, One in Three.
Oh, grant us endless length of days
  In our true native land with Thee. Amen.

An Act of Consecration to the Sacred Heart of Jesus
(May be made during Benediction.)

Most Sweet Jesus, Fountain of Love, Father of Mercies and God of all Consolation, Who hast vouchsafed to open to us, wretched and unworthy sinners, the unspeakable riches of Thy Heart! In thanksgiving for the innumerable favors conferred upon us and upon the rest of mankind, and especially for the institution of the most Holy Eucharist, and in order to repair all the injuries done to Thy most Loving Heart in this Mystery of infinite Love, we entirely devote ourselves and all that is ours to this most Sacred Heart of Thine, promising that we will promote the worship of Thy Divine Heart as far as may be in our power.

We humbly beg, therefore, of Thine infinite goodness and clemency, that Thou wilt vouchsafe to receive this holocaust in the odor of sweetness, and that as Thou hast granted us Thy plentiful grace to desire and make this offering, so Thou wilt also grant us the same to enable us to fulfill it.

People: Amen.

Priest: O most tender Heart of Jesus, grant that we may love Thee.

People: And for no other reward than that we may love Thee more and more.

Tantum Ergo

Tantum ergo Sacramentum
  Veneremur cernui;
Et antiquum documentum
  Novo cedat ritui;
Praestet fides supplementum
  Sensuum defectui.

Genitori, Genitoque
  Laus et jubilatio,
Salus, honor, virtus quoque
  Sit et benedictio:
Procedenti ab utroque
  Compar sit laudatio. Amen.

Priest: Panem de caelo praestitisti eis.
   (*T. P.* Alleluia.)
People: Omne delectamentum in se
   habentem. (*T. P.* Alleluia.)

Oremus.

Priest: Deus qui nobis sub Sacramento
   mirabili, passionis tuae memoriam reli-
   quisti, tribue, quaesumus, ita nos corporis
   et sanguinis tui sacra mysteria venerari, ut
   redemptionis tuae fructum in nobis
   jugiter sentiamus. Qui vivis et regnas in
   saecula saeculorum.
People: Amen.

Down in Adoration Falling
(*English version of the* Tantum Ergo.)

Down in adoration falling,
   Lo! the sacred Host we hail;
Lo! over ancient forms departing,
   Newer rites of grace prevail;
Faith for all defects supplying
   Where the feeble senses fail.

To the Everlasting Father,
   And the Son who reigns on high,
With the Spirit Blest proceeding
   Forth from Each eternally,

Be salvation, honor, blessing,
  Might and endless majesty. Amen.

Priest: Thou hast given them Bread from Heaven. (*P. T.* Alleluia.)
People: Containing in Itself all delight. (*P. T.* Alleluia.)

Let us pray

Priest: O God, Who in this wonderful Sacrament hast left us a memorial of Thy Passion, grant, we implore Thee, that we may so venerate the sacred mysteries of Thy Body and Blood as always to be conscious of the fruit of Thy Redemption, Thou Who livest and reignest forever and ever.
People: Amen.

The Divine Praises

Blessed be God.
Blessed be His Holy Name.
Blessed be Jesus Christ, true God and true Man.
Blessed be the Name of Jesus.
Blessed be His Most Sacred Heart.
Blessed be His Most Precious Blood.
Blessed be Jesus in the most Holy Sacrament of the Altar.

Blessed be the Holy Spirit, the Paraclete.

Blessed be the great Mother of God, Mary most Holy.

Blessed be her Holy and Immaculate Conception.

Blessed be her glorious Assumption.

Blessed be the Name of Mary, Virgin and Mother.

Blessed be St. Joseph, her most chaste spouse.

Blessed be God in His Angels and in His Saints.

Laudate Dominum

(May be sung at the close of Benediction.)

All: Adoremus in aeternum Sanctissimum Sacramentum.

Choir: Laudate Dominum omnes gentes; laudate eum omnes populi.

People: Quoniam confirmata est super nos misericordia ejus; et veritas Domini manet in aeternum.

Choir: Gloria Patri et Filio et Spiritui Sancto.

People: Sicut erat in principio, et nunc, et semper, et in saecula saeculorum. Amen.

All: Adoremus in aeternum Sanctissimum Sacramentum.

AUTHORITIES ON VISIONS AND MIRACLES

Authorities on Divine Manifestations

ST. THOMAS AQUINAS—". . .On the part of the person seeing it, whose eyes are affected in the same way as if they really saw outwardly (existing) flesh, or blood, or a child, whilst yet no change has happened on the part of the Sacrament. . . . Nor is there any deception in this. . . because such impression is divinely made in the eyes to figure forth a particular truth—*i.e.,* to show that the Body of Christ is truly under this Sacrament. Even so Christ, without deception, appeared to the disciples going to Emmaus. For Augustine says that when our figure is referred to a particular signification, it is not an untruth, but a special figure of the truth. And since in this manner no change takes place on the part of the Sacrament, it is clear that Christ does not cease to exist under the Sacrament during such apparitions."

—*Summa Theologica,* III, Q. 76, art. 8.

FR. FREDERICK W. FABER—"There are two sorts of apparitions, and both of them true, supernatural and divine, the handiwork of God. First of all, God by His absolute power can make such an impression on the senses of His servant, that while others see the absolute whiteness, roundness, thinness and quality of the sacramental species, he beholds a beautiful vision of the Babe of Bethlehem presented to him by the Divine Will; and it is no deceit; for as St. Augustine says, a fiction which is referred to as signification is not a falsehood, but a figure of the truth. Or again, when it is God's will that a whole multitude should behold the vision, instead of miraculously impressing their senses, He may please to change all the accidents of the Host, its commensurable quantity excepted—which is the root and support

of all the accidents—and may convert them
into this appearance; and thus the laws of
the Sacrament are not injured, falsified, or
fundamentally disturbed, the dimensions
remaining inviolate. . .These, as appearances
of flesh and blood, are astounding evidences
of the truth of the Blessed Sacrament; these
apparitions of an infant are literally types,
figures of its spirit, manifestations of its
sweetness, disclosures of the devotional
character which is apt to form."

—*The Blessed Sacrament,* p. 206.

Authorities on Human Assent to Divine Manifestations

HOLY SCRIPTURE—"Amen, amen, I say to
you, he that believeth in Me, the works that
I do, he also shall do; and greater than these
shall he do. . .He that loveth Me, shall be
loved of My Father; and I will love him, and
will manifest Myself to him."

—*John* 14:12,21

POPE BENEDICT XIV— "Though an
assent of Catholic faith be not due to them
(miracles), they deserve a human assent
according to the rules of prudence by which
they are probable and piously credible."

ST. ALPHONSUS LIGUORI—"The bad are ready to deny miracles as the good are to believe them; as it is a weakness to give credit to all things, so, on the other hand, to reject miracles which come to us attested by grave and pious men, either savors of infidelity which supposes them impossible to God, or of presumption which refuses belief to such a class of authors. We give credit to a Tacitus, a Suetonius, and can we deny it without presumption to Christian authors of learning and probity? There is less risk in believing and receiving what is related with some probability by honest persons and not rejected by the learned, and which serves for the edification of our neighbor, than in rejecting it with a disdainful and presumptuous spirit."

—*The Way of Salvation,* p. 93.

ST. AUGUSTINE—"When a miracle is made known, however striking it may be in the very place where it happened, or even related by those who witnessed it, it is scarcely believed, but it is none the less true."—*De Utilitate Credende,* p. 75.

ST. BERNARD—"These revelations are not the work of man; and no mortal will understand them unless love has renewed in his soul the image and likeness of God."

—*Missus est,* p. 182.

ST. FRANCIS DE SALES—"When facts are related that teach and edify us, we should not believe that the proofs upon which they rest are entirely false and worthless. 'Charity believeth all things,' which is to say it does not easily believe *that one lies.* And if there be no sign of falsehood in what is represented to her, she makes no difficulty in giving it credence, especially when it relates to anything which exalts and praises the love of God towards men, or the love of men towards God, the more so as *Charity* is the sovereign queen of virtues, takes pleasure, after the manner of princes, in those things which tend to the glory of her empire and domination. Supposing, then, that the narrative be neither so public nor so well attested as the greatness of the wonder would seem to require, it loses not for that its truth."

—*Introduction to the Devout Life,* p. 90.

If you have enjoyed this book, consider making your next selection from among the following . . .

Prices subject to change

Moments Divine—Before Bl. Sacrament *Reuter* 10.00
Raised from the Dead—400 Resurrection Miracles 18.50
Wonder of Guadalupe. *Johnston* 9.00
St. Gertrude the Great. 2.50
Mystical City of God. (abr.) *Agreda*. 21.00
Abortion: Yes or No? *Grady, M.D.* 3.00
Who Is Padre Pio? *Radio Replies Press* 3.00
What Will Hell Be Like? *St. Alphonsus* 1.50
Life and Glories of St. Joseph. *Thompson* 16.50
Autobiography of St. Margaret Mary 7.50
The Church Teaches. *Documents* 18.00
The Curé D'Ars. *Abbé Francis Trochu* 24.00
What Catholics Believe. *Lovasik* 6.00
Clean Love in Courtship. *Lovasik* 4.50
History of Antichrist. *Huchede*. 4.00
Self-Abandonment to Div. Prov. *de Caussade* 22.50
Canons & Decrees of the Council of Trent 16.50
Love, Peace and Joy. *St. Gertrude/Prévot* 8.00
St. Joseph Cafasso—Priest of Gallows. *St. J. Bosco*.... 6.00
Mother of God and Her Glorious Feasts. *O'Laverty*.... 15.00
Apologetics. *Glenn* 12.50
Isabella of Spain. *William Thomas Walsh*. 24.00
Philip II. P.B. *William Thomas Walsh*. 37.50
Fundamentals of Catholic Dogma. *Ott*. 27.50
Creation Rediscovered. *Keane* 21.00
Hidden Treasure—Holy Mass. *St. Leonard* 7.50
St. Philomena. *Mohr* 12.00
St. Philip Neri. *Matthews*. 7.50
Martyrs of the Coliseum. *O'Reilly*. 21.00
Thirty Favorite Novenas. 1.50
Devotion to Infant Jesus of Prague. 1.50
On Freemasonry *(Humanum Genus). Leo XIII* 2.50
Thoughts of the Curé D'Ars. *St. John Vianney*. 3.00
Way of the Cross. *St. Alphonsus Liguori* 1.50
Way of the Cross. *Franciscan* 1.50
Magnificent Prayers. *St. Bridget of Sweden* 2.00
Conversation with Christ. *Rohrbach* 12.50
Douay-Rheims New Testament. 16.50
Life of Christ. 4 vols. P.B. *Emmerich*. 75.00
The Ways of Mental Prayer. *Lehodey*. 16.50

Prices subject to change.

Old World and America. (Grades 5-8) *Furlong* 21.00
Old World and America Answer Key. *McDevitt* 10.00
Miraculous Images of Our Lord. *Cruz* 16.50
Ven. Jacinta Marto of Fatima. *Cirrincione* 3.00
Ven. Francisco Marto of Fatima. *Cirrincione*, comp. 2.50
Is It a Saint's Name? *Dunne* 3.00
Prophets and Our Times. *Culleton* 15.00
Purgatory and Heaven. *Arendzen* 6.00
Rosary in Action. *Johnson* 12.00
Sacred Heart and the Priesthood. *de la Touche* 10.00
Story of the Church. *Johnson et al* 22.50
Summa of the Christian Life. 3 Vols. *Granada* 43.00
Latin Grammar. *Scanlon & Scanlon* 18.00
Second Latin. *Scanlon & Scanlon* 16.50
Convert's Catechism of Cath. Doct. *Geiermann* 5.00
Christ Denied. *Wickens* 3.50
Agony of Jesus. *Padre Pio* 3.00
Tour of the Summa. *Glenn* 22.50
Three Ways of the Spir. Life. *Garrigou-Lagrange* 7.00
The Sinner's Guide. *Ven. Louis of Granada* 15.00
Radio Replies. 3 Vols. *Rumble & Carty* 48.00
Rhine Flows into the Tiber. *Wiltgen* 16.50
Sermons on Prayer. *St. Francis de Sales* 7.00
Sermons for Advent. *St. Francis de Sales* 12.00
Sermons for Lent. *St. Francis de Sales* 15.00
St. Dominic's Family. (300 lives). *Dorcy* 27.50
Life of Anne Catherine Emmerich. 2 Vols. 48.00
Manual of Practical Devotion to St. Joseph 17.50
Mary, Mother of the Church. *Documents* 5.00
The Precious Blood. *Faber* 16.50
Evolution Hoax Exposed. *Field* 9.00
Devotion to the Sacred Heart. *Verheylezoon* 16.50
Chats with Converts. *Forrest* 13.50
Passion of Jesus/Its Hidden Meaning. *Groenings* 15.00
Baltimore Catechism No. 3. . . . . 11.00
Explanation of the Balt. Catechism. *Kinkead* 18.00
Spiritual Legacy of Sister Mary of the Trinity. 13.00
Dogmatic Theology for the Laity. *Premm* 21.50
How Christ Said the First Mass. *Meagher* 21.00
Victories of the Martyrs. *St. Alphonsus* 13.50

Prices subject to change.

Practical Comm./Holy Scripture. *Knecht.* (Reg. 40.00) . 30.00
Sermons of St. Alphonsus Liguori for Every Sun. 18.50
True Devotion to Mary. *St. Louis De Montfort* 9.00
Religious Customs in the Family. *Weiser.* 10.00
Sermons of the Curé of Ars. *Vianney* 15.00
Revelations of St. Bridget of Sweden. *St. Bridget* 4.50
St. Catherine Labouré of/Miraculous Medal. *Dirvin* 16.50
St. Therese, The Little Flower. *Beevers* 7.50
Purgatory Explained. (pocket, unabr.) *Fr. Schouppe* 12.00
Prophecy for Today. *Edward Connor* 7.50
What Will Hell Be Like? *St. Alphonsus Liguori* 1.50
Saint Michael and the Angels. *Approved Sources* 9.00
Modern Saints—Their Lives & Faces. Book I. *Ball* 21.00
Our Lady of Fatima's Peace Plan from Heaven 1.00
Divine Favors Granted to St. Joseph. *Pere Binet* 7.50
Catechism of the Council of Trent. *McHugh/Callan* . . . 27.50
Padre Pio—The Stigmatist. *Fr. Charles Carty* 16.50
Fatima—The Great Sign. *Francis Johnston* 12.00
The Incorruptibles. *Joan Carroll Cruz* 16.50
St. Anthony—The Wonder Worker of Padua. 7.00
The Holy Shroud & Four Visions. *Fr. O'Connell* 3.50
St. Martin de Porres. *Giuliana Cavallini* 15.00
The Secret of the Rosary. *St. Louis De Montfort* 5.00
Confession of a Roman Catholic. *Paul Whitcomb* 2.50
The Catholic Church Has the Answer. *Whitcomb* 2.50
I Wait for You. *Sr. Josefa Menendez.* 1.50
Words of Love. *Menendez, Betrone, etc.* 8.00
Little Lives of the Great Saints. *Murray* 20.00
Prayer—The Key to Salvation. *Fr. M. Müller.* 9.00
Alexandrina—The Agony and the Glory. 7.00
Life of Blessed Margaret of Castello. *Fr. W. Bonniwell* . 9.00
St. Francis of Paola. *Simi and Segreti.* 9.00
Bible History of the Old and New Tests. *Schuster* 16.50
Dialogue of St. Catherine of Siena. 12.50
Dolorous Passion of Our Lord. *Emmerich* 18.00
Textual Concordance of the Holy Scriptures. PB 35.00

At your Bookdealer or direct from the Publisher.
Toll-Free 1-800-437-5876   **Fax 815-226-7770**
Tel. 815-229-7777   **www.tanbooks.com**

Prices subject to change.